THE TEACHING GUARANTEE

MAKING A DIFFERENCE

Ken Darvall

Copyright © 2024 (Ken Darvall)
All rights reserved worldwide.

No part of the book may be copied or changed in any format, sold, or used in a way other than what is outlined in this book, under any circumstances, without the prior written permission of the publisher.

Prepublication Data Service
P.O. Box 159, Calwell, ACT Australia 2905
Email: publishaspg@gmail.com
http://www.inspiringpublishers.com

 A catalogue record for this book is available from the National Library of Australia

National Library of Australia The Prepublication Data Service

Author: Ken Darvall
Title: The Teaching Guarantee: Making a Difference
Genre: Non-fiction

Paperback ISBN: 978-1-923250-10-9
ePub2 ISBN: 978-1-923250-11-6

Table of Contents

Dedication vii
Foreword ix
Acknowledgements xvii
Abbreviations xix
About the Author xxi
Introduction xxiii

Section 1: Culture 1
1. Growth Mindset 2
2. Standards 4
3. Responsibility 6
4. Purpose 8
5. Beliefs 10
6. Values 13
7. Traditions 16
8. Key Stakeholders 18
9. Relationships 20

Section 2: Leadership 23
10. Vision 24
11. Expectations 26
12. Action-Oriented 29
13. Solutions-Focused 31
14. Kaizen 34
15. Team of Leaders 36
16. Integrity 38
17. Decisiveness 40
18. Visibility 42

Section 3: Strategy 43
19. Context 44
20. Initiatives 46

21. Planning 48
22. Implementation 50
23. Evaluation 52
24. Critical Actions 53

Section 4: Organisational Structure 57
25. Systems 58
26. Procedures 61
27. Processes 64
28. Personnel 68
29. Conflict 72
30. Development 75

Section 5: Communication 81
31. Who 82
32. What 85
33. How 88
34. When 92
35. Why 95
36. Articulation 98

Section 6: Projects 101
37. Need 102
38. Initiative 105
39. Actions 108
40. Experiences 112
41. Opportunities 116
42. Evidence 120
43. Celebrations 124

Section 7: Reputation 129
44. Targets 130
45. Timelines 135
46. Evidence 139
47. Impact 143

48. Performance 147
49. Success Results 151
50. Success Inspiration 155
51. Promotion 159

Section 8: Focus 163
52. Student Engagement 164
53. Curriculum for Choice 167
54. Learning Environment 170
55. Individualised Support 174
56. Emotional Wellbeing 178
57. Community Involvement 181
58. Technology Integration 185
59. Extracurricular 189
60. School Expertise 192

Dedication

This book is dedicated to Tema International School (TIS), where making a difference is inherent in its ethos. Mr and Mrs Adjavon founded TIS and have been supported by their children, Anthony, Catherine, Cecilia, and Frances, since its opening on 3 October 2003.

The TIS Family, comprising students, parents, staff, and alumni, continue to make the school proud through their initiatives and achievements.

Tema International School is a family school and a unique experience.

https://tis.edu.gh

Foreword

Making a difference isn't just about big gestures. It's in the little things, the service we render, the lives we touch, and the community we build together. - Surama King

With great honour and deep respect, I write the foreword for *The Teaching Guarantee: Making a Difference*, a reflective memoir by Dr Ken Darvall, recounting his transformative leadership as Principal at Tema International School (TIS). This book captures not only the essence of a visionary educational leader but also serves as a guide for those aspiring to make a profound impact in the field of education.

When Dr Ken joined our community in 2015, the TIS Secondary School campus served Grades 7 through 12. His visionary alignment with the school's Founding Family's vision catalysed the inclusion of a vibrant Primary School campus, reflecting his commitment to a comprehensive educational approach. Over the years, his strategic expansions and initiatives have significantly reshaped the academic landscape at TIS, illustrating a pragmatic, detail-oriented, and student-centred philosophy.

A pivotal element of Dr Ken's tenure has been his deep resonance with the foundational vision established by the Founders of TIS. This harmonious relationship has been instrumental in propelling the school's mission forward. Dr Ken's leadership has been a living embodiment of the Founders' dreams, seamlessly integrating their values into the school's evolving culture and curriculum, ensuring that every new initiative aligns with and builds upon their original aspirations. His approach has always been to weave these foundational principles into our daily educational practices, ensuring that the Founders' legacy continues to thrive and guide TIS's journey.

Dr Ken's leadership style is characterised by a steadfast pursuit of excellence and an intolerance for mediocrity—a philosophy that might be daunting to some but is deeply rooted in his core principles. He famously insists, "Excellence is not an act, but a habit," a statement that has become a guiding mantra for our institution, pushing us to strive beyond the bounds of complacency.

Under his mentorship, I have experienced profound personal and professional growth. Dr Ken encouraged me to venture beyond my comfort zone, supporting my journey from speaking at international educational conferences to pursuing my M.Ed at the University of the People. His belief in continuous development and his support for addressing challenges like dyslexia with a creative perspective have been particularly impactful. He often says, "Your unique perspective adds invaluable depth to your writing," which has encouraged me to embrace my unique qualities as strengths.

Dr Ken's dedication extends beyond administrative leadership, evident in his daily interactions with our school community. Known for being the first to arrive on campus and his morning walks, greeting each student by name, he practises his philosophy that "to lead is to serve; to serve is to care." This personal engagement is a testament to his deep respect for the community and his commitment to educational excellence.

The Teaching Guarantee: Making a Difference is more than just a memoir or a manual; it is a manifesto for transformative education. Throughout the book, Dr. Ken emphasises the importance of giving one's personal best and fostering a culture where striving for excellence through encouragement and support is the norm. His commitment to service is profound, endorsing students' initiatives and actively engaging in them, ensuring they come to fruition. He believes strongly in action over words, a principle evident in his decision to dedicate the proceeds from his book, **The Teaching Guarantee: Every Day is Different,** to the **Transforming Lives Project.**

As someone fortunate enough to work closely with Dr Ken, I know that his educational philosophy and leadership approach have influenced my professional practices and enriched my understanding of what it means to truly be an educator. His methods, characterised by innovation, integrity, and insight, challenge us to rethink traditional approaches and inspire us to embrace a future where every educational act is a deliberate step toward making a meaningful difference.

I invite you to delve into the pages of ***The Teaching Guarantee: Making a Difference*** with an open heart and a willing mind. Prepare to be inspired, challenged, and transformed by Dr Ken's resourceful guidance. It is a journey well worth taking that promises to enlighten and invigorate all who embark on it.

This book is a guiding light for all educators and leaders committed to fostering environments that elevate, empower, and educate. Dr Ken's journey and the principles he advocates offer a compelling blueprint for anyone dedicated to making a significant impact in the educational sphere. May this book inspire you as much as Dr Ken's leadership has inspired those of us fortunate enough to have been his colleagues and students at TIS.

Here's to educational encounters that are as intentional and meaningful as Dr Ken Darvall's teachings to us all. As you turn the pages of ***The Teaching Guarantee: Making a Difference***, I encourage you to absorb Dr. Ken Darvall's profound insights and to actively apply them in your context, whether you are a school leader, administrator, or teacher. Each chapter offers knowledge and a call to action, urging you to make a difference wherever you find yourself. Let this book inspire you to take note, reflect, and enact the lessons learned, thereby transforming your educational environment and impacting the community you serve. This journey is not just about reading; it's about changing lives—one student, teacher, and community at a time. Embrace this opportunity to make a lasting impact, and join us in the noble quest of shaping futures through dedicated and insightful educational practice.

The Teaching Guarantee: Every day is different. Every school is different. Every student is different. So, as a teacher or principal, make a difference. **- Dr Ken Darvall**

At Tema International School (TIS), service is a value we discuss and live and breathe. It is deeply embedded in our core values, shaping the experiences of our students across the Primary Years Programme (PYP), Middle Years Programme (MYP), and Diploma Programme (DP). Over the years, our students have embarked on various service projects, each reflecting their diverse interests and the breadth of their impact. These projects have significantly influenced both themselves and the wider community. From donating learning supplies and organising food and book drives to renovating libraries, building schools, paying hospital fees, and constructing vital infrastructure, such as boreholes and toilet facilities, our students have left an indelible mark on the lives of many beneficiaries.

The International Baccalaureate (IB) program at TIS is not just about academic excellence, it's about making a difference in the world. The program incorporates Service as Action, the Community Project, and Creativity, Activity, Service (CAS), fostering a comprehensive understanding of service learning that aligns closely with the curriculum. These components are central to the IB philosophy and TIS's core values, enabling students to engage critically and compassionately with local and global issues and make a tangible impact on the world around them.

I would like to take this opportunity to mention just a few of the outstanding and impactful service projects at Tema International School (TIS) that integrate the SDGs and IB principles.

1. **The Akorlikope Project:** Started by the IB Class of 2012, this sustained CAS service project lasted nine

years. Each DP class from 2012 to 2021 contributed to the development of the Akorlikope community by providing basic educational needs and raising funds to complete a school building, library, headmaster's office, playground, bathroom, and canteen. In 2022, this project successfully concluded with the infrastructure handed over to Mr. Stephen Dodze, the caretaker/headmaster of the school, and the Ghana Education Service. Congratulations to all our DP students from the IB Class of 2012 to the IB Class of 2021. **(SDG 4: Quality Education)**

2. **Operation Smile (NGO):** Operation Smile Ghana is the country's largest provider of cleft care. The IB Class of 2024 raised over $3,000 to cover the total cost of corrective surgeries for three patients: Seraphine Aklasu, Albert Arthur, and Blessing Ebu Asabea. **(SDG 3: Good Health and Wellbeing)**

3. **Flamestar by Samra:** In 2021, two Grade 8 girls initiated a community project called Flamestar. They raised GHC 6,000 to construct a placenta pit at the Jericho Health Centre in Ashaiman. This project aims to support the clinic in effectively disposing of biological waste. **(SDG 3, 6: Good Health, Clean Water and Sanitation)**

4. **SaniFlush CAS Project:** A group of students from the DP Class of 2024 undertook a CAS project called SaniFlush. They raised approximately GHC 30,000 to construct a six-unit washroom facility, purchase toiletries, and provide a polytank to Ashaiman No. 2 JSS, a local school within the Ashaiman Municipal region. **(SDG 6: Clean Water and Sanitation)**

5. **EcoAid Project:** Led by a group of students from the DP Class of 2023, the EcoAid Project raised GHC 60,000 to refurbish the Boys Dormitory at the Echoing Hills Village, which accommodates 21 children with physical and mental spectrum abilities. **(SDG 10: Reduced Inequality)**

6. **Operation Replay:** In 2022/2023, six students (three DP and three MYP) initiated the Operation Replay

community project. They raised GHC 19,000 to refurbish and install a playground at the Tetteh Ocloo School for the Deaf, highlighting the importance of play in the lives of all children. **(SDG 3: Good Health and Wellbeing)**
7. **Spectrum Connect:** Two DP students engaged in a CAS project called Spectrum Connect, collaborating with the HopeSetters Autism Centre. They organised a Fun Day of activities and experiences for children from the centre and raised approximately GHC 20,000 to support the HopeSetters Autism Centre. **(SDG 3: Good Health and Wellbeing)**
8. **Bibliotheque Saint Juene:** A community project led by three MYP students raised GHC 15,000 to refurbish the St. John's Academy library in Ashaiman Bethlehem. The team contributed by donating furniture and textbooks to enhance the learning experience. **(SDG 4: Quality Education)**
9. **Do Great Things:** A group of students from the DP Class of 2022 initiated the Do Great Things CAS project. They raised $8,000 in collaboration with the KJM Foundation to construct a borehole in Fotobi, Eastern Region, providing potable drinking water to the community. **(SDG 6: Clean Water and Sanitation)**
10. **Unite To Light Ghana Initiative:** Initiated by a group of alumni, led by Nubuke Gadzekpo Amoah, in collaboration with the IB Class of 2020, students from the IB Classes of 2021 to the present have dedicated themselves to growing the project. The project focuses on sustainability and clean energy, raising awareness about the importance of solar energy and the detrimental effects of fossil fuel light. Over the past five years, 4000 LED solar Luke lights and 200 solar power banks have been distributed in Ghana, benefitting areas without electricity. The success of this project was made possible through collaboration with various organisations and individuals. **(SDG 7: Affordable and Clean Energy)**

FOREWORD

The Impact of Service Learning

Through these diverse projects, TIS students learn the value of empathy, the importance of sustainability, and the impact of their actions on the world. They develop project management, teamwork, and problem-solving skills, essential for their future careers and personal growth. Moreover, these experiences encourage a lifelong commitment to service, preparing students to be the change-makers of tomorrow.

The dedication of TIS to service learning not only enriches the lives of its students but also sets a profound example for educational institutions globally. As we have seen through numerous case studies, service is a core component of the IB programs and a crucial value at TIS. Schools must expose their students to the challenges in their communities, countries, and the world. This exposure is the only way to promote peace, equality, equity, and development. By fostering an environment where service is seamlessly integrated into the educational framework, we are developing compassionate, action-driven citizens. This commitment is the only guarantee for a brighter future—a principle dynamically exemplified by TIS's varied service initiatives over the years. The transformative power of education and its role in shaping a better tomorrow cannot be overstated.

The positive impact of our students' service initiatives at TIS is truly remarkable. These projects showcase their passion and dedication to effecting meaningful change in the world. We commend their efforts and express our sincere gratitude to all those involved, including our supportive community members. Special thanks go to the founding family, our co-founders Mrs Comfort Adzo Adjavon and the late Mr Alphonse Ayite Adjavon, whose vision continues to inspire us, as well as Cecilia Ajavon-Oppan and Frances Ajavon-Okudzeto; our school management, and our Principal, Dr Ken Darvall; along with the committed and energetic CAS-SA team—Grace Ameyibor, Abigail Ahiadorme,

David Difie, and Mawuli Zonyrah. By embracing service as a fundamental value, our students not only transform lives but also uphold the core promise of our institution: to actively contribute to a better world. This commitment is our "guarantee to making a difference."

Surama King,
CAS & Events Coordinator,
Tema International School
www.tis.edu.gh
Tema, Great Accra. Ghana, West Africa
Friday, 22 April 2024

Trustee, Creative Director - **The Children's Heart Foundation Ghana**
www.africadyslexia.org
www.thechildrensheartfoundationghana.org

Phone Number: +233 244 615255
Email: surama.king@gmail.com
YouTube Channel: https://youtube.com/@suramakking
Instagram: https://www.instagram.com/suramaking
LinkedIn: https://www.linkedin.com/in/surama-king-4b8651b7

Acknowledgements

I thank Surama King, TIS CAS and School Events Coordinator, for her willingness to write the foreword to this book. Surama is everywhere and everything at TIS, but she is also the consummate team player. Making it happen through actions and change has been her calling card since I have known her at TIS. She is an inspiration, counsellor, and mentor to all.

The length of my time at Tema International School (TIS), Ghana, explains the constant references to the opportunities and experiences at **T**his **I**ncredible **S**chool. TIS is a story worth telling.

To Mummy and Co-Founder, Mrs Comfort Adjavon, and Founding Family Members, Mrs Cecilia Ajavon-Oppan (General Manager), Mrs Frances Ajavon-Okudzeto (Deputy General Manager), I am grateful for you allowing me to be part of the TIS Family. It has been an honour.

Other key team members with whom I work closely: Eddy Torkornoo (Administrator), "AB" Abraham Anum-Quaye (Transport Manager), Yvonne Tagoe (MYP Coordinator), Jacob Lumumba (PYP Coordinator), Richard Domey (DP Coordinator), Gabriel Atseku (Sports Coordinator), Setor Adih (Girls Hostel Coordinator), Dennis Akortah (Boys Hostel Coordinator), Louis Welagaamo (PP & ATL Coordinator), Rita Fianko (Admissions), Alex Tetteh (School Maintenance Officer), Gina Mensah (Reception), Norah Kepomey (Uniforms and Accounts), Kobina Quansah and George Hagan (Accounts), Jerry Darko (Deputy MYP Coordinator), Eric Fudzagbo (Deputy DP Coordinator), Angela Quaye and Priscilla Annan (Deputy PYP Coordinators), Saviour Yevugah (G6 teacher), Grace Ameyibor (SA Coordinator), David Difie (Dukies Coordinator), Abigail Ahiadorme (ASA Coordinator), Mawuli Zonyrah (CASSA), Drs Kwekuma and Sally Yalley (School Doctors), Irene Koree, Kodzo Agbeko, Edward Kumah-Noi, Margaret Agbeli, Nathaniel

Attah and Ebeneza Asime (Heads of Department), Takasi Nyande and David Bayitse (IT), Eunice Aryee (University Guides Head), Sophia Dumakor (Head of Catering), Regina Owusu (Head of Infirmary), Ben Atter (Janitorial Team Leader) and Anthony Tenudze (Mr Everywhere Man), thank you and your teams for your support and dedication. To all other incredible TIS staff who make TIS the school it is today, continue to help TIS fly higher.

I am forever grateful to Mrs Dr Sylvia Boye for her continuous and unwavering support. Along with Mummy, Mrs Comfort Adjavon, these two are the grand dames of Ghana education for their impact over the decades. Other board members, Anis Haffar, Kwaku Sakyi-Addo, Audrey Gadzekpo, and Joe Oheming have always been supportive during my tenure. To our alumni, students, and parents, thank you for your support and for making TIS great.

Importantly, although not explicitly mentioned here (a project in itself), I am grateful for all the people I have met and worked with over the past 50 years: students, staff, parents, and community members who form part of my experiences and fond memories. These other school communities with whom I still hold cherished memories are: Five Mile Tree Public School; Collingullie Public School; Illabo Public School; Woodford Dale Public School; Weilmoringle Public School; Collarenebri Central School; Moree Public School; Hastings Public School; Al Zahra College (all New South Wales); Al Jazeera Academy (Qatar); Star Mountains Institute of Technology International School (Papua New Guinea); and, King Faisal School (Saudi Arabia.)

My orphan siblings, James, Phil, Cath, and Tric, have been important parts of my life throughout.

Most of all, thank you, Jan, for your love and patience.

Appreciate, value, and contribute to the teaching guarantee by making a difference often, if not daily.

Ken

Abbreviations

ASA	After School Activities
CAS	Creativity, Activity, Service
DP	(International Baccalaureate) Diploma Programme
ELL	English Language Learning
ESL	English as a Second Language
IB	International Baccalaureate
IGCSE	International General Certificate of Secondary Education
MYP	(International Baccalaureate) Middle Years Programme
MTSS	Multi-tiered System of Support
PYP	(International Baccalaureate) Primary Years Programme
Q&A	Questions and Answers
SDG	(United Nations) Sustainable Development Goals
SEL	Social and Emotional Learning
TIS	Tema International School (Ghana)

About The Author

Dr Ken Darvall has 50 years of educational leadership experience covering all educational sectors in Australia and overseas, including primary, secondary, and international schools, training organisations, international business colleges, school quality assurance reviews, and tertiary study abroad programs.

Complementing his extensive practical experiences, Dr Ken Darvall holds a range of relevant tertiary qualifications. These include a Teaching Certificate and Diploma in Teaching (Goulburn CAE), Bachelor of Arts and Masters of Educational Administration degrees (UNE), Diploma of Aboriginal Education (Armidale CAE), and a Doctorate of Education (CSU).

For the past two decades, Dr Ken Darvall has been dedicated to establishing and leading IB World Schools. His leadership roles include serving as the Academy Director at Al Jazeera Academy, Doha (PYP, MYP, DP); Education Director at Al Zahra College, Sydney (PYP, MYP, DP); Principal at SMIT International School, Tabubil (candidate PYP and MYP); and Primary School Principal at King Faisal School in Saudi Arabia (PYP). Currently, he is the Principal at Tema International School, Ghana (PYP, MYP, DP).

Ken enjoys sports coaching, music, educational technology, and research. He reviews books for Corwin and is a ManageBac Community Ambassador.

His first book, *The Teaching Guarantee: Every Day is Different*, was published in 2023.

Introduction

The Teaching Guarantee: Every Day is Different was published in 2023 to mark my 50 years in education. I now repeat the opening paragraph of the introduction of that book.

Since serving as the Teacher-in-Charge of Five Mile Tree Public School at Crooked Corner (New South Wales, Australia) in May 1973, I have coined a few sayings about school experiences that have rung true everywhere I have been. These include:

- The teaching guarantee: every day is different.
- Everyone is unique: one size does not fit all.
- A school is a school is a school.
- (As a teacher or principal), make a difference.

However, I must point out that making a difference is not just a responsibility or requirement in schools but for all organisations. While the responsibility is critical for the leader, other stakeholders are also responsible for making a difference in their organisation. While my background is in school education, the key points should also be transferable to other industries.

I have enjoyed making a difference at the various schools in which I have been involved with many of my colleagues at each of these schools. Elsewhere, some of my favourite projects have included driving the momentum, community approval, and the necessary organisational restructuring to establish the Primary Years Programme (PYP), the Middle Years Programme (MYP) and the Diploma Programme (DP) in schools. I have also ensured the successful authorisation of IB World Schools over the past 20 years. As a Quality Assurance Team Leader, I enjoyed leading organisational performance reviews in 42 schools across northern New South Wales.

School projects that met specific school needs were the Weilmoringle Heritage Project (1986), a local Indigenous studies program that focused on exploring and recording local history of the Muriwari tribe; the Collarenebri school-based courses, particularly my Aboriginal History course for Grade 10, which was approved by the NSW Board of Studies (1989); the Moree Kinder Start Program (1991-1993), a special Indigenous program for local students to minimise cultural barriers to their formal start to primary schooling; and the Moree District GAT Program (1992 - 1993), a program for talented and gifted students across Grades 3–6. The AJA Special Education Unit (2007-2008) provided opportunities for students with special needs (autism spectrum, et al.) who were not provided any options to enrol in international schools in Doha. The SMITIS Lighthouse School Project (2013) was an initiative for local and district schools to improve school education in the Star Mountains region of Western Province in Papua New Guinea. Programs included establishing a district principals' collaborative network, supply of musical instruments, and district school sports initiatives. The King Faisal School Learning Centre (2014-2015) enabled three key initiatives at KFS: during school time, underachieving students were withdrawn for periods of one week at a time to work intensively on their areas of weakness (English, Arabic, maths); outside school hours, staff could undertake training and professional development to enhance their effectiveness as teachers (for example, English proficiency, teacher training modules, IB program workshop sessions); and during school breaks or designated periods (for example, the first and last weeks of a term), providing IB workshops for staff from Saudi schools (KFF/IB partnership).

My TIS footprint covers the full implementation of ManageBac as a learning management system, although it was used before my arrival for only the CAS program. Over time, three other technology platforms that were implemented were OpenApply for school admissions, Kognity, an online source for secondary digital textbooks, and AssessPrep, as a source for online assessments.

Introduction

These systems ensured a smooth and speedy transition to online learning when COVID closed schools. At the time of my interview for the vacant Principal's position in 2015, I proposed implementing the IB Middle Years Programme, and establishing a Primary School with the Primary Years Programme as the obvious progression for TIS. The successful implementation of each Programme has certainly been a source of pride for everyone involved. Amalgamating two student leadership bodies, the SRC and Prefect system, into the Student Council, simplified and strengthened the school's student leadership structure. In a similar way, the monthly Bulletin and fortnightly newsletter were amalgamated into the weekly TIS Bulletin. At the time, no one understood how there would be enough information to communicate weekly. Essentially, this publication is an important historical record of what happens at TIS. Providing ID clarity for the school to articulate its tipping points (family school, opportunities, the four pillars, and the TIS DNA). Finally, the establishment of TIS as a Duke of Edinburgh International Award Centre was such a natural fit for this incredible school, allowing students to gain its various awards (Bronze, Silver, and Gold) through their consistent involvement in ASAs and service activities.

What I have come to realise over the past year is that the above changes were predominantly leadership-driven to address identified school needs. Examples of making a difference at TIS are spread throughout this book and the big difference at TIS is its culture drives changes through its actions. As I say, it is the TIS way. With a growth mindset culture and a Kaizen approach to continuous improvement, change is embraced with enthusiasm. It is the challenge to improve what we do.

So, there are three key messages from this book:

First, make a difference by addressing issues or problems through change to make the school or organisation more effective. Please start with the most pressing problem and resolve it effectively, and not with a band-aid solution. Develop a team culture by continuing to make these differences.

Second, strong, quality leadership is crucial to making a difference effectively by addressing the hardest issues to resolve, rather than the easiest. Unpleasant decisions will garner adverse commentary and criticism, but stay strong if your actions will improve the status quo, particularly student learning outcomes.

Third, as the TIS DNA illustrates, a strong school culture exemplifies what making a difference is all about. Strong, quality leadership over time will establish a robust, proactive school culture that encourages its stakeholders within an environment of a team of leaders. Once you experience it, nothing is more enjoyable because things happen without prompting. It's hard work, but the rewards are greater and more satisfying.

I have set this book out by breaking the process down, with each key element comprising its own chapter. I aim to make it practical by providing ideas for addressing different aspects. I have also suggested areas for change that may apply to your school or organisation in the final chapter ("Focus").

My intended outcome is to encourage schools and their leaders to make their mantra, "Making a Difference." I have enjoyed the experience over 50 years and thoroughly recommend it to you.

Peace, love, and happiness.

Ken Darvall
20 May 2024

THE TIS DNA

www.tis.edu.gh

SECTION 1

CULTURE

Culture is a school's heart and soul, defining beliefs, values, customs, celebrations, and reputation.
— *Ken Darvall*

1
Growth Mindset

The key to a successful school or organisation is the prevailing culture.

While many critical components define a culture, the most important is a growth mindset. The characteristics of a growth mindset are embracing change, persisting in the face of setbacks, seeing effort as the path to mastery, learning from criticism, and finding lessons and inspiration in the success of others. These elements will promote transformation.

On the contrary, a fixed mindset avoids challenges, gets frustrated or gives up easily, thinks potential is predetermined, takes criticism personally, and feels threatened by others' success. These characteristics will support a maintenance or status quo culture, where change is difficult and transformation is another word in the dictionary.

Therefore, a growth mindset culture will view change as continuous improvement, in which problems are challenges to improving performance and reputation.

From experience, a growth mindset promotes readiness. This was evident at TIS when COVID started shutting down the world in March 2020. Pre-COVID, we enjoyed a digital environment with a learning management system and access to digital textbooks and other online resources. Each student used their laptop at school. During school closures, as the secondary school was a boarding school, we considered it safer for students to remain at school with restricted visiting and strict protocols rather than for them to return home.

While many schools struggled to move from in-classroom to online learning, we implemented effective systems within one week and timetables were operating as normal. It wasn't perfect, with internet and power outages causing havoc and student engagement issues for those who missed the social side of the classroom. Although students relied on their devices, they were very happy to return to the classrooms when lockdowns were lifted.

Critically, learning loss was limited because it was "business as usual" due to our growth mindset mentality.

2

Standards

Standards must be articulated and flexible (in terms of resetting them due to continuous improvement) and they will only be achieved by authentic teamwork, collaboration, and empowerment.

The standards to which I refer here are those that the school sets for its community and may be in terms of performance, attendance, dress, grievances, and communication. The standards will be in areas of school life that the school community deems important. One standard that I insist in schools is the 48-hour rule for communication. Too often, very small issues that should be resolved at the time of occurrence are left to fester into a major incident that should have been resolved months earlier. Establishing an open-door policy has been a standard that I have always adopted. Making parents book appointments may provide some order to the day, but it may also frustrate an irate parent who needs to be heard now. In 99.9% of cases involving irate parents, the matter is resolved by removing the time-delay strategies any organisation can establish to stifle issues. I detest bureaucracy, so I expect processes to be streamlined so that issues can be addressed at the time and not allowed to "fall off the table."

Establishing a standards culture in a school demonstrates an empowered school with high expectations regarding standards. Such a culture exists at Tema International School (TIS) where each performance or event must be better than the previous year's event. Two key events are Founders' Week and the Annual Play.

TIS Founders' Week celebrates its Founders, Mr and Mrs Adjavon, along with their children and families (Founding Family). Grade 11 students establish a program for the week, and separate teams are responsible for the daily activities. This responsibility becomes part of the students' CAS program. On Founders' Day, a concert is always followed by a special luncheon. Other significant events, such as Teachers' Day and International Day, are held on a separate day of this week so it is quite an exhausting celebration. But each year, the organising committee goes one better than the previous year in its planning, preparation, and rules based on fun, sensibility, and a celebration of our Founders. I have witnessed nine of these celebrations and a higher standard is evident yearly.

The Annual Play is performed around the second weekend in November each year. The school's 10th-anniversary performance of *The Lion King* in 2013 was also hailed as the benchmark. However, subsequent productions had unique aspects that qualified each as the best performance. Each performance identifies a couple of new stars who would be the least you expect to perform and surprise you with their magical performances. The 15th-anniversary performance was an adaptation of *Beauty and the Beast* at the National Theatre in Accra. It was simply stunning in every possible way. It would not have been out of place if performed on Broadway, New York. People stopped talking about *The Lion King*. It would be impossible to improve on the *Beauty and the Beast*. But a new standard is set by selecting unknown plays and producing a magical performance in which students excel in all their characterisations. Yes, the performance is better each year and the students ensure that the standards' culture is evident to all. To impress further, students take on the crew responsibilities for staging, music, costume, design, and makeup. Each year, I am mesmerised by these talented students and supporting staff. So, insist on a standards culture that empowers the school community to demonstrate and enjoy continuous improvement annually.

3
Responsibility

Another critical element in a strong culture is a sense of responsibility.

Employees (and employers) will have a list of responsibilities relative to their position within an organisation.

Key stakeholders may or may not have articulated responsibilities. Board of governors will, students will have rules and regulations, while parents may have either expectations or stated responsibilities regarding fees, uniforms, attendance, and behaviour.

However, there is a difference between position responsibilities and a sense of responsibility.

Position responsibility will determine performance, while a sense of responsibility will determine loyalty. For example, a staff member is responsible for submitting a leave form when absent. Yet, I have seen many teachers come to school when unwell out of loyalty to their students, as they don't want to disappoint them.

A sense of loyalty demonstrates that a person's role in the organisation is not just a job or responsibilities they have to do with minimal effort. They do it because of their pride in the organisation. They do it because they also believe in making a difference by what they do.

Loyalty means you complete the job no matter what it takes.

Responsibility is a commitment to the school's vision, mission, values, and beliefs.

Ideally, an organisation demonstrates shared responsibilities as it does with its values. In these instances, colleagues will support and encourage each other to achieve intended outcomes out of their sense of responsibility.

Establishing the Primary School Campus at TIS demonstrated a shared responsibility. It was a successful task because of the absence of existing Primary School traditions, in contrast to the established secondary school. For example, the intention from the start was the Primary School would be authorised as a PYP School within three years. Therefore, it was critical that potential staff had to be open-minded, risk-takers and not carry any baggage from a traditional teaching approach, if the inquiry learning model was to be implemented successfully. Recruitment focused closely on potential staff looking for a change who could implement a new teaching and learning model.

Before the opening of the Primary School, the new teachers were provided with four weeks of intensive training from our PYP Coordinator, Jacob Lumumba, a very experienced IB educator. What evolved was terrific! The new staff adopted a strong team approach and were enthusiastic to demonstrate all best practices of a PYP teacher and learning environment.

4
Purpose

The purpose of an organisation is vital for three reasons. Importantly, it provides the "why" an organisation exists. Second, it provides 'what' the organisation wants to achieve. Then, it provides 'how' it wants to fulfil its purpose.

The purpose sets the tone for an organisation as it explains its existence. Why did we start? What do we want to achieve? How will we do it?

The purpose must resonate with others and relate to their needs and wants. It's the organisation's purpose that attracts your stakeholders.

The purpose will create the culture of the organisation.

A school or organisation's mission statement typically states it purpose. It is a concise statement that communicates the reason for the organisation's existence and the fundamental objectives it seeks to achieve.

A well-crafted mission statement provides clarity and direction to guide an organisation's activities and decision-making processes. It often reflects the organisation's values, vision, and long-term goals. The mission statement serves as a guiding principle for the organisation and helps stakeholders, employees, and the public understand its purpose and what it aims to accomplish.

TIS Mission Statement

Tema International School seeks to:

- Provide an excellent and diverse education for all, irrespective of nationality, ethnicity, creed, or gender.
- Draw on the cultural diversity of the school community as a foundation for building universal human values.
- Develop the spirit of inquiry in all our students as a fundamental tool for encouraging critical thinking and stimulating intellectual development.
- Create a safe and supportive environment that promotes self-discipline, honesty, integrity, and excellence in learning.

We believe the young adults who graduate from TIS possess the knowledge and relevant skills to unlock opportunities and contribute meaningfully to their communities.

Our Annual Achievement Day and Graduation Ceremony are evidence of our purpose and what it strives to achieve. Fulfilling the purpose of the TIS Founders requires hard work, consistent and focused effort, and strong achievements.

5
Beliefs

An organisation's purpose will help define its beliefs.

Beliefs will provide the guideposts for an organisation's culture.

Tema International School has 14 statements of belief.

At TIS, we believe proof of evidence is essential and required to demonstrate commitment.

At TIS, we believe balance, by maximising opportunities and experiences to enhance learning and challenge oneself, inside and outside the classroom, is the key to success.

At TIS, we believe excellence is achieved by continuously improving your personal best in all endeavours through consistent effort, a positive attitude, regular reflection, balance, persistence, a growth mindset, and no excuses.

At TIS, we believe experiential learning allows our students to understand the theory in the classroom to practise across the real world, where personal experiences and reflections add meaning and purpose to each student while making the world a better place.

At TIS, we believe adequate sleep each night will enable students to feel rested in the morning and ready to function at their best to tackle their challenges for the day and tick off plenty of boxes along the way. We know it will affect their performance, health, appetite, attitude, and behaviour without adequate rest.

At TIS, we believe that integrity, or the lack of it, defines the individual and their reputation. We strive to display it as our badge of honour.

At TIS, we believe that success results from taking on new challenges by moving out of your comfort zone, ensuring consistency by avoiding complacency, understanding that performance requires balance, and reflecting on outcomes to set new personal best targets. After all, success is personal.

At TIS, we believe that through actions and service that demonstrate our commitment to the UN Sustainable Development Goals, we can make the world a better place. But we must be active and committed participants, not just vocal spectators.

At TIS, we believe that personal success is best judged by one's proficiency in demonstrating daily the 10 IB Learner Profile attributes: thinker, inquirer, reflective, caring, open-minded, communicator, knowledgeable, risk-taker, balanced, and principled.

At TIS, we believe that sport, as one of the four pillars for student balance and ensuing success, promotes teamwork, challenges personal best, and emphasises the importance of appreciating how to lose before knowing how to win.

At TIS, we believe that service, as one of the four pillars for student balance and ensuing success, provides a hands-on experience to how we can make the world a better place through action and an understanding that success comes from helping others grow and becoming empowered.

At TIS, we believe that the academics, as one of the four pillars for student balance and ensuing success, provide a theoretical lens for inquiry, critical thinking, and conceptual understanding, as well as the opportunity to demonstrate our knowledge and understanding across many areas of learning.

At TIS, we believe that culture, as one of the four pillars for student balance and ensuing success, develops and enhances the creative, artistic, and performing skills and talents in each student.

Welcome to the Leadership Incubator. At TIS, we believe the four pillars for student balance and ensuing success—academics, service, sport, and culture—provide a theoretical lens for inquiry, critical thinking, and conceptual understanding in a real-world context through action. Across all four pillars, TIS prides itself on the opportunities and experiences that enable graduates to develop and enhance leadership attributes and skills to make a difference and improve the world. As leaders, we create our footprints to ensure authenticity.

6
Values

(School) Values are the core principles or standards that guide a school community or organisation's behaviour, decisions, and actions. In other words, they're the school's moral compass. They are important because they help create a positive and inclusive school culture while also serving as a guide for students, teachers, and parents regarding what is expected in terms of conduct and attitude. Additionally, they can enhance student engagement and learning by promoting a sense of belonging and respect.

At TIS, we have nine core values:

Excellence
We facilitate quality teaching and learning with our wide range of resources to ensure that each community member reaches his or her peak of excellence.

International-Mindedness
We are conscious of global interconnectedness. Hence, we engage in activities that make it easy to fit into every environment, regardless of which part of the world we find ourselves. We pick a little bit of everything and pick everything when necessary.

Honesty
We live by this: "Honesty is the best policy."
PS: That is the truth.

Respect
We are aware of each other's feelings and develop healthy relationships amongst ourselves, which is critical for survival. We

treat our environment with care, knowing that sustaining it will benefit us all.

Critical Thinking
We promote the "seeing and listening beyond the surface" kind of analysis in and outside class to enable us to view concepts and theories from varied perspectives and, in the process, widen the scope of our knowledge.

Creativity
We do not take things simply for what they are. Instead, we take them for what they can be. It is in identifying potential and opportunity that innovativeness and imagination blossom.

Teamwork
We operate with the "alone, we can do so little; together, we can do so much" philosophy. Hence, we apply our knowledge to activities and group research, establishing collaboration and cooperation among students, teachers, and parents.

Transparency
Nothing stays behind the light; we bring everything into the light. We ensure that TIS knowledge is everyone's knowledge.

Service
We believe that "love has no meaning if it remains by itself, that it has to be put in action, and that action is service." Therefore, we participate in community service to express our love for humanity and the sustenance of our environment.

Once established, can the core values change?

Schools and organisations change over time due to various factors. What is critical is that the values reflect what is important and relevant to the school.

At TIS, we have celebrated its 20th anniversary in 2023, and this is an excellent moment to reflect on our core values to ensure relevance. For example, integrity has been the most important word at the school over the past four years. So, should the core value of honesty be rebadged as integrity? Should responsibility become an additional core value? These two questions are for broader discussions to ensure ownership.

7
Traditions

School traditions are regular activities, events, or practices unique to a school. They can range from annual productions to daily practices like morning assemblies or school songs. They are important for a few reasons.

Sense of Belonging
Traditions can help students, teachers, and parents feel part of a community and promote a sense of school spirit.

Continuity
They provide a sense of continuity and predictability, which can be comforting.

Identity
They contribute to the school's identity and culture, making it distinct from others.

Memories
They create lasting memories and experiences for everyone involved.

There are a few steps to create or enhance school traditions.

Identify the Purpose
What's the goal of this tradition? It might be to build community, celebrate achievements, or maintain a historical connection.

Involve Stakeholders
Get input from students, staff, parents, and alumni. They might have great ideas or perspectives on what will work best.

Consider Diversity
Make sure the tradition is inclusive and respectful of all students' cultures and backgrounds.

Start Small
You don't have to plan a massive event right away. A small, well-executed tradition can be just as meaningful.

Iterate and Evaluate
After the tradition takes place, get feedback. What worked? What didn't? Use this to improve and evolve the tradition over time.

However, it is important to remember it's not just about creating traditions but maintaining and enhancing them.

On the other hand, traditions can provide a huge barrier to change. For example, when TIS looked at implementing the Middle Years Programme (MYP) to replace the International General Certificate of Secondary Education (IGCSE), it created great angst and division at the school. The IGCSE commenced at the school in 2005 and suited the traditional Ghanaian school culture of "chew and pour." However, there was a huge disconnect between the IGCSE and DP when students progressed from one to the other. MYP implementation addressed this issue and provided continuity between it and DP. Initially, the take-up of MYP was not authentic until staff could see the obvious benefits of implementing MYP authentically.

8
Key Stakeholders

In any school, there are several key stakeholders, each with a vested interest in the school's success.

At TIS, the key stakeholders are the founding family, students, teachers and staff, parents and families, senior management team, board of governors, local community, and our cherished alumni.

Founding Family
The co-founder and her family continue their involvement in the school to ensure their vision and values remain evident and guide future actions.

Students
They are the primary reason TIS exists! Their success is the primary goal.

Teachers and Staff
They are on the front lines of educating and supporting students every day.

Parents and Families
They play a crucial role in their child's education. Without parents, there are no students!

Senior Management Team
This includes the principal, general and deputy general managers, administrator, financial controller, program coordinators, and the hostel coordinators. This team makes key decisions about the running of the school.

Board of Governors
The board ensures the effective management of the school and plays a key role in developing, approving, and reviewing the mission and strategic vision of the school.

Local Community
Local businesses and community organisations often have a stake in the school's success.

Alumni
Our former students are involved in fundraising, mentoring, and other support. Our alumni are a unique group in my experience. Apart from school events with different alumni guests, we have many alumni visiting the school unannounced. Individually or in small groups, they enjoy saying hello to staff and students and admiring all the changes that have occurred at TIS since their graduation. The inspiration and wisdom they provide to our students are priceless.

At TIS key events, each program will usually involve representation from each stakeholder group. For example, at the 2023 Achievement and Graduation Day, there was an alumni speaker from 2013 and a parent speaker from the graduating cohort. All other stakeholder groups either performed or were involved in handing out awards.

9
Relationships

Relationships are the heart of a school community.

Relationships are like the glue that holds everything together.

Strong relationships foster a sense of belonging and trust. When everyone feels valued and heard, they're more likely to engage and contribute positively.

Better relationships also lead to better communication. This is the key for everything from resolving conflicts to sharing ideas.

Let's not forget collaboration. When relationships are strong, people are more willing to work together, whether it's on a school project or a new initiative.

Strong relationships with teachers and peers can boost students' academic success and socio-emotional development.

In a nutshell, everything works better when relationships are strong.

A growth mindset promotes positive relationships. At TIS, the home of Fast and Furious, something is happening all the time. This culture of achievement also promotes strong relationships as success will be difficult without strong relationships and a sense of common purpose. Striving to achieve an intended outcome strengthens the relationship of teams and communities. It reflects a sense of "we can do this!"

Emphasising a team/collaboration approach to tasks is always desirable. Having key team members to promote and support its purpose will only ensure success.

There should be a sense of equality across the staff hierarchy so that any member of staff who is enthusiastic and has a sense of responsibility can contribute to a project, whether they are middle management or the school cleaner.

Three examples demonstrating the emphasis on strong relationships with the TIS community during its 20th anniversary (2023/2024) were the Primary School end-of-unit celebrations, which are always a full-house event at the Primary School Campus; the Founders' Week events when former staff, parents, and alumni joined current staff, students, and parents to celebrate This Incredible School; and the MYP Evaluation, which recognised the power of its culture and the strong and proactive relationships within the school community.

SECTION 2

LEADERSHIP

Leadership is foremost about teamwork, vision and goals, being a role model, being a problem-solver, and trying to bring the best out in everyone.

— *Ken Darvall*

10
Vision

If a school or organisation has a strong culture, its vision, values, and leadership significantly contribute to its culture.

If there is an undefined culture, then leadership will be responsible for establishing it. To do so, the key elements of leadership in this chapter must also be intertwined with the cultural elements discussed in the previous chapter.

A vision is like a compass for a school or organisation. It provides a clear long-term direction to help everyone understand the purpose and goal of their work. It's a big-picture statement that guides decision-making and inspires team members to achieve a common goal. Without a vision, actions can become disjointed and uncoordinated, limiting the potential for success.

At TIS, our vision is:

To be an International School of choice nurturing world-class citizens responsive to the needs of society.

The above example ticks essential boxes for me. It's concise and not verbose, articulating three specific, timeless goals. In a single sentence, the direction of the school is set: to be an international school of choice. The two goals are (1) nurturing world-class citizens and (2) being responsive to the needs of society.

What does this mean at the ground level? TIS requires a reputable international school curriculum. In this case, the school has sought and achieved IB World School status and is authorised to offer the Primary Years Programme (PYP) for P-6, the Middle Years

Programme (MYP) for Grades 7-10 and the Diploma Programme (DP) for Grades 11-12. In doing so, TIS provides a world-class education for its students, with all graduating students attending universities worldwide. Additionally, service is a compulsory requirement of each IB programme, so each student undertakes service activities each year at TIS, selected and driven by the students.

The statement is timeless due to three essential variables – reputation, performance, and societal values and/or needs. These variables will be affected by internal and external factors that must be addressed purposefully as they arrive.

11
Expectations

Schools need to communicate the expectations of the key stakeholders: students, staff, and parents. The following expectations are what I consider to be important in a school.

Students
There are five aspects where high standards are always expected: performance, behaviour, presentation, communication, and participation.

Performance
Student performance is expected to at least equal or exceed their natural ability. Regardless of a child's natural ability level, each student is expected to put their best effort into every task they attempt.

Behaviour
Students are expected to: be ready to learn; be in the right place at the right time (with the right gear/equipment); respect staff, students, and visitors; respect their own and the property of others; apply the best effort to each activity; and be honest.

Presentation
Students are expected to be in the correct school uniform (and worn properly) on school grounds or in the wider community representing the school.

Communication
"Sooner rather than later" is the standard for all communications. If there is an issue or concern, then individuals must communicate this issue or concern to the relevant party. All issues and concerns are expected to be addressed quickly (48-hour rule).

Participation
Students are expected to participate in all class/school activities. Failure to do so raises the question of commitment.

Staff
Staff must always be professional. Their actions and behaviours reflect themselves, their professional colleagues, and the school.

Staff will demonstrate their professionalism in different ways.

Their commitment to excellence and high standards will be reflected in the performance of their duties. Students' performance and their results are considered a reflection of teaching staff performance.

Their efforts to ensure effective communication between colleagues, students, and parents. All communication must reflect a "sooner rather than later approach" (48-hour rule). Email is the preferred form of communication. Staff should copy in their Head of Department, Program Coordinator, and the Principal.

Their establishment of strong home–school relationships.

Their loyalty and commitment to the school are always and without exception.

Their ability to **make a difference** to the school as a result of their professional and personal contributions by **value-adding in their individual areas of expertise**.

Their prompt follow-through on all tasks and requirements for which they are responsible.

Their participation in extra-curricular activities and school events.

Parents

All parents are expected to support the policies and ethos of the school.

By email, they should promptly communicate any issues with the class teacher or relevant staff member (48-hour rule) on working days (Monday - Friday, 8 am - 4 pm).

They will demonstrate courtesy and respect with school staff and other parents.

They will attend parent/teacher interviews and information sessions and participate in school functions and events.

They will pay school accounts according to the set time frames and ensure their children return to school within the set timeframes.

12
Action-Oriented

Leadership is about leading the way rather than managing the status quo.

"Comfort zone" is a great destination—for retirement! For a leader, it is a tell-tale sign that you have already reached your expiry date.

Especially in a school or organisation with no culture or one that is undefined, the leader must be action-oriented if making a difference is the intent. In this instance, the leader will start from scratch in establishing a culture to include all the critical elements in the first section.

The key difference between a strong and indifferent organisational culture is that quality leadership over time has established a strong culture that exudes success. In the case of an undefined culture, strong and sustained leadership will be required to define, create, and establish a strong culture with full stakeholder take-in. Depending on the circumstances, it may be a career-defining moment and, hopefully, with a positive outcome for all.

Regardless of the circumstances, the leader's determination, insight and experience will enable the leader to prepare a list of actions designed to demonstrate the importance of change and a new direction to ensure "buy-in" from key stakeholders. This evidence of action will enable the leader to identify and enlist important supporters to influence others in the school or organisation.

What leaders in this situation must remember is that talk is cheap. In a school with an undefined culture, stakeholders will enjoy and support leaders who "walk the talk" rather than just "talking the talk." Over time, the lack of action by previous leaders has created an undefined organisational culture.

The next chapter outlines the second component of being able to make a difference.

13

Solutions-Focused

Being action-oriented as a leader is critical, but it must be purposeful.

To ensure purposeful action, it must be solution-focused. In other words, the action will address a critical issue preventing a school or organisation from moving forward.

The best way to do this is at the start of tenure, the leader announces that he requires "intelligence." This intelligence will provide the data to identify the organisation's strengths and future directions in two simple questions. What do we do well? What must we do better?

Reassure the stakeholders that there are no right or wrong answers. For the leader, the data will identify the trends that are, hopefully, triangulated by observation or other sources of evidence.

For instant success, the leader should prioritise the areas for improvement, and immediately address the most important issue and try to resolve it within a few weeks. This will establish your most valuable strength: credibility.

But don't stop after your first success. Keep moving down your list so that your credibility becomes your reputation. Along the way, target and involve your key supporters in planned actions so that they are also promoting the same message.

Remember two things: change is not easy, and very few people ever like leaving their comfort zone for the promised land. A leader's skillset and experience will be fully displayed during these times of change. Also, be mindful that if a desired action fails, see if you can tweak the action to resolve the original point of weakness.

A critical moment in the history of Tema International School was the implementation of the IB Middle Years Programme (MYP). TIS opened in 2003 and by 2005 it was authorised as an IB World School to offer the Diploma Programme (DP) and a Cambridge exam centre, so that the IGCSE could be offered.

The advantage of the IGCSE was that it offered an external examination at the end of its program. This was a good experience for DP students who had to complete external exams at the end of their program in Year 12. Most parents had completed the IGCSE when they went to school. As parents and the community described, the IGCSE was "chew and pour"—memorise and regurgitate.

The disadvantage of the IGCSE was its disconnect from the Diploma Programme (DP). For the IGCSE students moving onto DP, it was like stepping from Earth to Mars. The terminology was different, the learning approach was different, the assessment was different, and the subjects were different. These students struggled for up to a semester to settle fully into the Diploma Programme.

I had witnessed this same disconnect in other schools and realised the only way to address this issue was to establish the Middle Years Programme (MYP) to replace the IGCSE. I recall at the interview for the principal's position at TIS in May 2015, I stated a priority would be to establish MYP for the important reason of removing the disconnect that impacted students when they transitioned to the Diploma Programme in Grades 11 and 12.

The reluctance to change from IGCSE to MYP was obvious for several years, including after MYP authorisation. In the end, the MYP consultant brought the issue to a head when it was pointed out that TIS had to make a decision. It was either IGCSE or MYP, but not both.

Fortunately, MYP introduced eAssessments at the end of the Middle Years Programme, eliminating its critical weakness—no formal end-of-programme examination system. Importantly, TIS agreed to drop IGCSE after TIS was authorised to offer MYP.

This defining moment marked a shift for TIS, moving from a fixed mindset to a growth mindset.

The benefits of this momentous change have been witnessed over the past five years since authorisation. These changes were obvious during our school's 2023 MYP programme evaluation covering the COVID-19 years.

14

Kaizen

Kaizen is a Japanese word meaning improvement. In the business world, it refers to activities that continuously improve all functions and improve all employees, from the CEO to the assembly line workers. A Kaizen approach has many benefits, including improved productivity, employee engagement, quality improvement, cost savings, and improved customer satisfaction.

If we transfer the Kaizen approach from the business world to a school setting, the benefits can be improved teaching methods, increased student engagement, enhanced collaboration, efficiency in operations, and the promotion of a growth mindset. In a nutshell, these are the keys to an efficient and effective school.

At TIS, Kaizen is a tradition without using the word! At TIS, Kaizen enables our challenge mentality.

Each year, it is understood that any event or activity must be better than the previous one. Usually, this is impossible.

In 2013, during the school's 10th anniversary celebrations, TIS raised the bar and wowed the audience with its adaptation of the Broadway award-winning musical *The Lion King* at the National Theatre in Accra. Over the next five years, all you heard was *The Lion King*. It was the benchmark. I did not witness the production, but I heard the unending accolades.

When I arrived in 2015, Sarafina was the annual production at the school and I thought it was brilliant. In fact, stunning. What you must realise is that students "own" the production. They are the cast but also the crew, and there are student directors for each aspect of a school production. Each year, the annual performance was different and superb. One or two students, the most unlikely you could imagine, played key roles each year.

In November 2018, as part of the 15th anniversary celebrations, TIS performed an adaptation of *The Beauty and The Beast*. WOW! The National Theatre performance made you feel like you were watching it on Broadway. It was simply mesmerising! *The Lion King* was no longer the benchmark. It was now *Beauty and the Beast*.

The annual performances have continued; each was better than the last. How do you improve on *Beauty and the Beast*? By taking a different genre and setting, students take ownership of the performance and understand that what they do must be better than last year's performance. And it is! Students take up the challenge with delight and confidence.

The Kaizen approach is evident in everything we do at TIS. Importantly, it occurs without using the word, Kaizen.

15
Team of Leaders

Leadership can often be seen as a single entity. We refer to specific individuals as leaders or demonstrating leadership attributes.

A successful school or organisation must have effective, strong, focused, collaborative, empathetic, and charismatic leadership. Whatever the adjective, the common perception is that leadership is individualistic, as per the expression, "it's lonely at the top of the tree!"

Yet, a leader can't do everything. Many may try, but an individual leader can achieve only so much. The best leaders are collaborative and rely on teams to ensure successful outcomes. Relationships are everything. So is delegation, since a leader can develop future leaders by sharing and delegating responsibilities to develop future leaders.

In essence, the successful organisation comprises a team of leaders under the watchful eye of their leader-coach. While most organisations have a senior management team, the concept of a team of leaders goes beyond the role of the senior management team. The team of leaders will be assigned project leaders of teams that are established to implement an initiative or priority.

A team of leaders can be a gamechanger for a school or organisation because it promotes diverse perspectives, shared responsibility, increased motivation, skill development, and improved decision-making.

I refer to TIS as the home of Fast and Furious, regarding the opportunities and experiences we offer our students. It is not rocket science to realise that a team of leaders is required to ensure that these opportunities and experiences continue to benefit our students and provide leadership opportunities to our staff and students.

The TIS annual performance is a classic example of a team of leaders. Since the annual performance production occurs over four months, leadership development is an intensive experience. Similarly, service projects in MYP and DP will also demonstrate this team of leaders' approach to achieving the intended outcome/s.

I see three main benefits of adopting a team of leaders approach. First, the approach enables key projects to be undertaken simultaneously. Second, it provides critical leadership development experiences to potential leaders. Third, it builds a group of leaders through a succession plan.

16
Integrity

Integrity: what you do when no one is watching.

Integrity = Principled (IB Learner Profile attribute)

Integrity = Trust

Integrity = (your) Reputation

Integrity is the badge of honour everyone should wear on their sleeve.

Integrity is the most important word at TIS. As I tell students, if everyone demonstrates integrity as a habit, then there is no need for rules, as everyone will go about their day "doing the right thing."

Often, the trouble is that there are few role models for others to follow. Unfortunately, too many consider integrity as a light switch, where you can turn it off and on when you want to. This is not integrity but just kidding yourself.

People depend on friends they can trust. Lose that trust, and you lose your friends. In times of need, we need people whom we can trust. Otherwise, the help becomes a hindrance.

Most importantly, integrity becomes your reputation. Your reputation will stand with you through life. What reputation do you want to have or be known by?

At a school level, all stakeholders need to be accountable for their integrity within the school. No one should be trying to harm, damage, or diminish a school's reputation through their decisions and actions. People who demonstrate their integrity will only enhance their personal or organisation's reputation through their actions.

At TIS, our Integrity Code is:

TIS, as a family school that provides unique experiences, embodies a spirit of integrity and respect for others, which are central to each member's personal, academic, and ethical development.

As a TIS family member, I promise to uphold and demonstrate its values and protect the school's reputation. I make this pledge in the spirit of honour and trust.

Behaviour and actions are considered in relation to the integrity code. If a student is bullying others, how do these actions relate to the integrity code? How do these actions impact on the school's reputation and values?

17

Decisiveness

One key leadership attribute that often goes missing is decisiveness.

Decisiveness is at one end of the decision-making spectrum. Bureaucracy is at the other end.

Is decisiveness lacking in the collaborative decision-making process? Hopefully not. If the process requires a meeting outcome, decisiveness is still apparent. However, if a committee approach to decision-making operates, then bureaucratic fumbling, and likely no decision, will be the norm.

Decision-making is a key responsibility of leadership. Yes, it is important to make the best decision based on context, purpose, and intended outcome.

Decisiveness is easier in low-level decision-making. It becomes complicated when the impact of a decision on stakeholders increases. This is when a leader must clearly understand the priorities of each stakeholder group in the organisation. Acting against these priorities usually disenfranchises the stakeholder group and causes leadership headaches.

Technology has promoted the need for decisiveness. In the era of snail-mail technology, postal delays and mishaps ensured a lapse in decision-making time. On the contrary, email has promoted decisiveness, where an answer or decision is almost expected by reply email.

Often, the strategic leader has predicted issues and has already discussed key matters with the senior management team so that an agreed decision has already been made. Thus, when a decision is required, it has already been made and can be communicated with confidence.

However, leaders know that a new policy or decision is only as good as the day it is made. This is not a weakness but a reflection of changing circumstances. Remember the COVID-years? During the first 12 months, new decisions were being made hourly. Putting out an announcement was likely to be redundant within the hour and a new decision would be required to replace the previous one. These were unpleasant and complex times in any school or organisation.

Most people appreciate decisiveness so that they can continue with their planning and actions. Otherwise, it becomes frustrating to most parties if a bureaucratic mindset is adopted when no decision is made.

18
Visibility

A leader requires visibility, which in turn promotes access.

Visibility is similar to decisiveness insofar as at the polar extreme is bureaucracy (and the make-an-appointment approach).

Leadership visibility sends some clear messages to all stakeholders.

When leaders are visible and transparent, it fosters **trust** within the school or organisation. Staff who see their leaders regularly are more likely to believe in their decisions and direction.

Visibility can **inspire** their teams. Seeing the dedication, hard work, and passion of leaders can motivate employees to strive for the same.

Visibility **enables open communication**. Approachable and present leaders can hear firsthand the challenges, ideas, and feedback from their team.

When leaders are visible, they demonstrate their **accountability**. Staff also see that leaders are doing their part and fulfilling their responsibilities.

Visible leadership helps define the culture of the school or organisation. It **sets the tone** for behaviour, work ethics, and values.

Importantly, leadership is not just about giving orders from behind a desk. It's about being present, involved and engaged with your team and stakeholders.

SECTION 3
STRATEGY

Strategy provides you with the guidance to set practical goals, the focus to help concentrate the resources, and clarity so that everyone knows their roles and direction.
— *Ken Darvall*

19
Context

Understanding the school context to which you are appointed (as a teacher, executive, or principal) should be a priority task. The school context will describe its unique features and detail information that reflects the school's educational, geographical, and social characteristics. It will usually state the school's key areas of strength and areas for improvement or further development. The school context will provide the meaning and understanding from which future plans and actions will be developed.

The context will provide you with the priorities for your planning and action. However, understanding the school's culture and ethos will reveal how to implement your plans and actions. Like students, each school is unique in its culture and ethos. Some schools will have empowered school communities, while others may have fractured school communities. I have worked in several different types of communities and have enjoyed their support very early in my tenure at each location.

The most important starting point for the newly appointed principal is identifying the most pressing issue. What is holding the school back? Effectively address the identified issue time-efficiently and you will enjoy many supporters because you are tackling the most important issues. It will be evident that you want to make effective change.

I must emphasise the importance of key stakeholders and developing a team of leaders.

It is important to identify the power brokers among the staff and parents and try to align them with your strategic plans. Use these power brokers to communicate your ideas and their support. Also, look at creating alliances with different sections of a school community so that you have a support base for any action or events that may require assistance.

Especially among staff, try to identify the change agents who can support you in communicating and supporting your plans for change. Ensure that any changes will benefit teachers most regarding the roadblocks they face. Early success will again be contagious and empower staff with a can-do attitude.

After you know that you are making a difference because of the successful changes that have resulted from your initiatives, I recommend belief statements that define your context. Use these statements to remind your school community about what is important to your school (or organisation). You can also use these belief statements to promote and market your school as points of difference.

The 14 TIS belief statements have been listed in Chapter 5, "Beliefs."

20
Initiatives

Once you have the context of an organisation, you can identify the initiatives that can make a difference. Here is why initiative and initiatives are critical to your strategy to make these differences.

Initiative is a critical attribute for any leader. A successful leader will present an initiative to address an issue, challenge, or opportunity by articulating why (it is important and what will be the outcomes), what (it is all about and the benefits), how (it will be implemented), when (it will be implemented), and who (will be involved). Ideally, initiatives will be encouraged by all stakeholders within the organisation.

Leaders must be solution-oriented. Issues will always arise for any leader. Rather than being reactive, the approach should always be proactive, thus, solution-oriented. Leaders should be strategic in outlook, so their solutions are looking to address future challenges and opportunities rather than known issues. For example, if schools rely on public or private transport for students to reach school, traffic delays will be inevitable at some time. This is a known (predictable issue), so there will be plans in place for when students arrive late. The late students are probably already frustrated and anxious, and parents may be concerned about their safety, so a very "calming" routine needs to be in place so that students can start their school day without distractions.

On the other hand, a growing locality indicates a likely increased student population for the school. The principal and school management team should start looking at how an increasing school population will impact the dynamics of the school and how it will mitigate the expansion with minimal disruption to the school's learning programs.

When it comes to initiatives, critical planning details, the importance of agency, sources of funding, and recognition are key factors.

Initiatives often need more detail to visualise their implementation. Three aspects are critical:

- Planning is key.
- Ensure the initiative addresses the articulated issues or opportunities.
- Set key targets throughout the implementation process to keep planning on track.

Schools should be dynamic organisations, so principals will encourage initiatives and innovation from all stakeholders to ensure agency, empowerment, authenticity, and transparency.

For schools, major initiatives are likely to benefit from a grant process. While the application process can be painful, addressing all requirements usually results in sufficient funding to implement the initiative. When successful with a grant application, the principal should always promote its success and advise the school community why the initiative is important, its timeline, the project coordinator, and the outcomes.

Lower-cost initiatives likely to be funded by parent bodies must also receive the same promotion and acknowledgement. Ensuring a proactive parent body that provides funding for their initiatives will always be invaluable to schools.

21
Planning

The first key to success is planning. The second key is preparation.

Planning is the key to your day, lessons, meetings, reporting, communications, and strategic direction. Everything.

Some key areas for planning will consume a lot of the leader's time. Essential planning that will occupy a significant amount of time will include:

Strategic planning: What are the school's priorities over the next three to five years?

Management planning: How do we implement the priorities set for the current year?

Financial planning: How do we fund all priorities and ongoing budget costs?

Personnel planning: Do we have the (right) staff to implement the programs for the current year?

Facilities planning: Do we have appropriate facilities to implement the programs for the current year?

Admissions planning: Do we have accurate vacancy details so that the admissions process can take place confidently?

Event planning: When will scheduled events and activities be held during the year?

Excursions planning: What trips will be approved for bookings, and when will they occur?

Curriculum planning: What are the curriculum priorities across the school and grades, and what are the timelines involved?

Equipment planning: According to the replacement cycle, what equipment will be replaced this year, and when will it occur, according to the school budget?

From the previous chapter, "Initiatives," some of a school's critical issues to address as a priority will come from the above planning areas. These initiatives should drive the school's short- to medium-term strategic directions. However, the two most important considerations will be identifying the top two or three (and no more) priorities to address and forming key teams to ensure the priorities are achieved within the set timeframe. The first few initiatives should be achievable in ten weeks or less to continue the momentum of moving forward at the school or organisation.

Generally, the key elements for the planning will be establishing effective small teams to drive the initiatives, identifying the key achievable outcomes (possibly identified in earlier surveys and discussions), choosing the timeframe, and addressing any costing matters. Importantly, please remember the old adage: keep it simple. This way, everyone will know the goal of the initiative, its rationale, implementation steps, the timeframe, and intended outcomes. As stakeholders identified the initiative as a top priority, there should be support from all stakeholders.

When identifying key team members to form the success team, choose members who are passionate about the focus, have a record for getting things done, are team players and influencers. Importantly, each member should be self-driven to ensure the goal(s), deadlines, and intended outcomes are met and achieved to the satisfaction of the school community.

22

Implementation

Six steps to a successful strategy implementation include communicating goals, team engagement, plan execution, staying agile, getting closure, and evaluation (see the next chapter.)

The keywords for implementation are simplicity, clarity, transparency, teamwork, engagement, and accountability.

Having determined the required initiatives and the planning, it's now time for implementation. This phase will determine the authenticity of the planning, but adapting the planning to address emerging issues should also be expected.

The planning team's leader should ensure focus and momentum, so communicating the goals of the implementation phase will be critical to ensure everyone is "on the same page." These goals should articulate the timeline, team members' roles, and key actions moving forward.

Team engagement is critical with the expectation that each team member wants ownership for the intended change/s. Assigning tasks that will take advantage of personal strengths or provide developmental opportunities for them. Team membership can provide critical personal and professional development for individuals and should be a priority for leaders.

The plan execution needs to tick boxes so all parties can sense action taking place. Communicate succinctly as you progress so that awareness is not an issue. Utilise personnel outside the team as required, but with the team's knowledge and support.

Staying agile refers to confronting emergent issues as they arise to avoid the process of stumbling. Amending and refining plans and processes must occur to address personal context issues. Initiatives are important and needed to address issues that appear "difficult" to overcome for whatever reasons. The increased credibility and gratitude will be obvious as obstacles are removed and progress is evident.

Getting closure and achieving initiative goals, preferably within the predicted timeframe, will be a celebration for all, pending the overall outcomes achieved. Three important associated outcomes should be a sense of ownership, especially for the implementation team, a sense of pride for the school community for addressing the issue and an increasing momentum for further change and action.

As mentioned earlier, the keywords for implementation are simplicity, clarity, transparency, teamwork, engagement and accountability. Ensuring simplicity regarding goals and actions, especially due to clarity and transparency, will ensure a smooth process. Effective teamwork will make the process enjoyable and manageable. It will also ensure team engagement which is critical for ownership. Effective teamwork will also demonstrate accountability which will be reflected by the ownership of the process and outcomes.

23
Evaluation

Evaluation is just as crucial as planning for any project or task.

The evaluation process is a reflection of what occurred and the outcomes achieved. Its importance lies in the lessons learned, actions to replicate in the future, and insights for future avoidance or refinement.

The evaluation and feedback from team members may be beneficial for future guidelines for project teams. The feedback may identify personal strengths or areas for future development. Feedback may also highlight an associated priority that needs to be addressed.

Seeking wider feedback may guide future teams in terms of communication, priorities, and processes.

Importantly, the evaluation process will always identify the evident strengths and areas for future development.

Evaluation and feedback should always be sought at different critical stages of any project to ensure transparency and accountability. This process should be characterised by simplicity and clarity to ensure meaningful responses that guide the process.

24
Critical Actions

Making a difference as a leader can be easy, complex, or even impossible. Some variables will determine the level of complexity, while leadership insight will influence the level of success in terms of outcomes. The final judgment of making a difference will be the final outcome of the actions taken. While success will be shared across the school community, disappointment will reflect poorly on the leader.

To avoid disappointment, note the following critical actions to be taken during the process.

Leadership insight will ensure success by having an awareness and understanding of the school's context. This understanding will help predict critical changes required within the organisation, best implementation strategies, and likely success members to be part of the implementation team. This insight will allow the team to take ownership of the process and advise the team, if required, if momentum has stalled.

Setting clear objectives for the planning initiatives and keeping strategies simple will ensure clarity and focus for the implementation team. Setting a realistic timeline to complete the process should be aligned with the process objectives. Keep the timeline short, ideally 30-60 days, so the focus does not drift or diminish. Avoid competing projects that may stall the change project and distract team members.

Involving key stakeholders in the project will develop a sense of community and empower the community for further change initiatives once success has been experienced. Use proactive supporters as team members to ensure momentum for the project. Keep in mind how this experience may develop the individual team members.

Develop specific action plans and enable a stepping-stone approach so that boxes can be ticked off along the way, maintaining team momentum.

Allocate resources required at any stage within the change process. There should be no excuses, as a project should only commence with the resources in place. A lack of resources, especially when promised, is a major morale-buster for the team and community. This needs to demonstrate better planning and impact on the duration of the process and its outcomes.

Monitoring progress will be an important responsibility for the team leader and the school leader, if not a team member. In this scenario, the school leader should take on a mentoring role so that the team leader develops as an important part of this process experience.

Communication and engagement will occur at two levels. At the first level, the implementation team will communicate and engage with the wider community to promote the empowerment of this change process. At the second level, the school leader will be on a similar trajectory with the key focus of maximising a successful outcome and process experience for the team and its members. Ultimately, it is about celebrating the change delivered, a successful process, and the team efforts of all involved.

Plans are sometimes imperfect, so we often refer to plans A, B, and C. Making changes along the way is critical if the required changes achieve the intended outcomes. Fostering a culture of adaptability must be an intended outcome while promoting a growth mindset to achieve our goals.

As mentioned in the previous chapter on evaluation, the team must review and update their strategic actions to reflect the context and circumstances that may arise. This is a consequence of fostering a culture of adaptability.

SECTION 4

ORGANISATIONAL STRUCTURE

Organisational structure is a key to success as it determines efficient communication, defines roles, and facilitates coordination among different departments and teams. Always ensure a responsive structure and never a bureaucratic model.
— *Ken Darvall*

25

Systems

The organisational structure of a successful school should incorporate various systems to ensure effective operation, communication, and continuous improvement. The following key systems should be evident within the organisational structure of a successful school.

Leadership and Governance
There will be clearly defined leadership roles and responsibilities. A governance structure will outline decision-making processes and responsibilities.

Teaching and Learning
The curriculum framework will be aligned with educational standards. There will be systems for lesson planning, delivery, and assessment. A professional development program will support teachers in enhancing their instructional practices.

Assessment and Evaluation
There are regular assessment practices to measure student progress. Assessment data will be analysed to inform instructional decisions. An evaluation system for teachers, administrators, and staff promotes professional growth.

Student Support and Wellbeing
Counselling services support students' social and emotional wellbeing. Student needs, including those related to special education, are identified and addressed. Health and safety protocols ensure a secure and supportive environment.

Professional Development

There are ongoing professional development opportunities for staff. Mentoring and coaching support educators in their growth. Continuous learning and improvement are valued within the school culture.

Communication

Clear communication channels for information flow between administration, teachers, students, and parents. Regular updates, newsletters, and announcements keep the school community informed.

Parent and Community Engagement

Programs and events involve parents in their child's education. Partnerships with the local community and businesses enhance resources and support.

Technology Integration

Technology is effectively used for teaching, learning, and administrative purposes. There is a system for maintaining and updating technology infrastructure.

Financial Management

Financial management practices are transparent and responsible. There are systems for budgeting, resource allocation, and financial reporting.

School Culture and Climate

A positive and inclusive school culture is promoted. There are systems for addressing behaviour, discipline, and conflict resolution.

Data Management

Efficient systems collect, analyse, and interpret data related to student performance, attendance, and other relevant metrics. Data is used to inform decision-making and drive improvements.

Strategic Planning and Improvement
Long-term strategic planning sets goals and objectives for the school. Continuous improvement processes involve stakeholders in identifying and implementing changes.

Emergency and Safety
There are clearly defined emergency response plans. There are regular drills and training on safety procedures for staff and students.

Facilities and Operations
Well-maintained facilities are conducive to learning. There are systems for managing school operations, including transportation, maintenance, and security.

Equity and Inclusion
Policies and practices promote equity and inclusion for all students. Systems address and mitigate achievement gaps.

By integrating and aligning these systems within the organisational structure, a successful school can create a cohesive and supportive environment that fosters student success, professional growth, and continuous improvement. Each system plays a crucial role in contributing to the overall effectiveness and positive school culture.

26
Procedures

Critical school procedures encompass a range of protocols and actions essential for maintaining a safe, effective, and well-functioning educational environment. The following key critical procedures should be evident in schools.

Emergency Response
Lockdown: Clearly defined procedures for responding to security threats.

Evacuation: Protocols for evacuating the school building during a fire or other emergency.

Emergency Communication: Established communication methods with students, parents, and staff during emergencies.

Crisis Management Plan
A comprehensive plan outlining steps to be taken in the event of a crisis, including roles and responsibilities of staff members.

Safety Drills
Regular drills for fire, earthquake, and other emergencies to ensure preparedness. Practice sessions for students and staff to familiarise themselves with emergency procedures.

Health and Wellness
Medical Emergencies: Protocols for handling medical emergencies, including access to first aid and medical personnel.

Medication Administration: Procedures for administering medications to students safely and controlled.

Security Measures
Controlled access to the school building, including visitor sign-in procedures. Surveillance systems and security personnel to ensure a secure environment.

Reporting and Responding to Bullying or Harassment
Clearly communicated procedures for reporting incidents of bullying or harassment. Defined processes for investigating and addressing reported incidents.

Student Arrival and Dismissal
Organised procedures for student drop-off and pick-up to ensure safety and efficiency. Clear guidelines for who is authorised to pick up students.

Attendance Tracking
Consistent procedures for tracking student attendance. Protocols for contacting parents or guardians when students are absent.

Curriculum and Teaching
Clear curriculum guidelines aligned with educational standards. Procedures for lesson planning, delivery, and assessment.

Discipline and Behaviour Management
Codes of conduct outlining expected behaviour for students. Procedures for addressing and managing student behaviour issues.

Special Education
Processes for identifying and supporting students with special education needs. Procedures for developing and implementing Individualised Education Plans (IEPs).

Communication
Regular communication plans with parents, including newsletters, emails, and parent-teacher conferences. Guidelines for communication between teachers, staff, and administrators.

Professional Development
Procedures for ongoing professional development for teachers and staff. Systems for mentoring and supporting new or less experienced teachers.

Budgeting and Finance
Transparent financial management practices. Procedures for budget development, resource allocation, and financial reporting.

Facility Management
Maintenance and cleaning procedures to ensure a safe and well-maintained physical environment. Protocols for addressing building issues or safety hazards.

Technology
Policies and procedures for responsible and safe use of technology. Systems for maintaining and updating technology infrastructure.

Parent and Community Engagement
Procedures for involving parents in school activities and decision-making. Protocols for engaging with the local community and building partnerships.

Data Privacy and Security
Procedures for safeguarding student and staff data. Compliance with data privacy regulations.

These critical procedures form the foundation for a well-functioning school environment. Regular review, training, and updates are essential to ensure that the procedures remain effective and aligned with the evolving needs of the school community.

27
Processes

Essential school processes are fundamental activities and routines that contribute to the effective functioning, safety, and success of the educational environment. These processes include administration, teaching and learning, student support, and overall school management.

Enrolment and Registration
Procedures for student enrolment include necessary documentation and information. Registration processes are available for new and returning students.

Curriculum Development and Implementation
The development of a curriculum aligns with educational standards. There are processes for implementing the curriculum and monitoring student progress.

Lesson Planning and Delivery
Teachers have procedures to plan and deliver effective lessons. Instructional strategies and materials are integrated.

Assessment and Grading
Tests, quizzes, and projects are systems for assessing student learning. Grading procedures and the timely communication of results are articulated.

Professional Development
There are processes for ongoing professional development for teachers and staff. Support is provided for educators to enhance their skills and stay current with best practices.

Student Support Services
There are procedures for identifying and addressing the needs of students requiring additional support. Special education services and accommodations are implemented.

Behaviour Management and Discipline
A code of conduct outlining expected behaviour has been implemented. Procedures address and manage student behaviour issues.

Parent-Teacher Conferences
Processes for scheduling and conducting regular parent-teacher conferences are explicit. Communication plans keep parents informed about student progress.

School Safety and Emergency Procedures
Emergency response plans have been implemented. Regular safety drills prepare students and staff for various emergency scenarios.

Attendance Tracking
There are procedures for recording and monitoring student attendance. Protocols for contacting parents or guardians regarding student absences are explicit.

Budgeting and Financial Management
There are processes for budget development, resource allocation, and financial reporting. Financial management practices ensure transparency and accountability.

Communication with Stakeholders
There are communication plans for regular updates to parents, staff, and the broader community. Procedures for handling public relations and media communications have been implemented.

Teacher Evaluation and Professional Growth
Evaluation processes assess teacher performance. Procedures provide feedback and support professional growth.

Facility Maintenance and Operations
Systems are in place for maintaining and cleaning school facilities. Procedures address building issues and safety concerns.

Technology Integration
Procedures are used to integrate technology into teaching and learning. Systems maintain and update technology infrastructure.

Data Management and Analysis
Procedures are used for collecting, analysing, and interpreting student data. The use of data informs decision-making and drive improvements.

Parent and Community Engagement
Processes involve parents in school activities and decision-making. There are protocols for engaging with the local community and building partnerships.

Professional Learning Communities (PLCs)
The creation of collaborative structures enables teachers to work together. Procedures encourage the sharing of best practices and addressing common challenges.

Strategic Planning
Long-term strategic plans that outline goals and objectives are implemented. Processes involve stakeholders in the planning and decision-making.

Graduation and Transition Planning
There are procedures for graduation ceremonies and transitioning students to the next educational level. There are support systems for university and career planning for high school students.

Collectively, these essential processes contribute to a school's smooth operation, supporting students' wellbeing and academic success while fostering a positive and effective learning environment. Regularly reviewing and refining these processes is crucial for adapting to evolving educational needs.

28

Personnel

No matter the context or position, almost everyone talks about getting the "best" person for the job. This approach makes sense. If you want the best, get the best!

Over the years, I have moved from the "best person for the job" to the "right person for the job." Why? In two words, the context.

Let me give you an example. Would an experienced principal of 25 years, with all their experience in the same middle-class school in England, be the best person for the Principal's position at TIS? In two words, probably not! I consider the person's likely strengths as their weaknesses: a fixed mindset. How would this leader handle the constant frustrations of power rationing, poor or no internet, and strict fiscal constraints? While different leadership experiences are invaluable, the same-same for 18 years can be described as doing the same thing 18 times. Flexibility, adaptability, and innovation will be the most desirable attributes, along with a coach mentality that can enthuse and develop his personnel. This is where the best person may not be the right person.

Personnel are key to an organisation's success. To attain success, personnel must work in effective teams with the express outcome of making it happen. Where possible, avoid a bureaucratic approach within the organisational structure. Keep the structure as flat as possible to promote leadership development at every opportunity. Employing staff using a right-person approach enables personnel strength and team versatility.

Highly effective organisations, including schools, prioritise certain essential requirements for their personnel to ensure success, productivity, and a positive work environment. These requirements span various aspects, from professional qualifications to interpersonal skills. The following can be considered essential requirements for personnel in a highly effective organisation.

Relevant Qualifications and Expertise
Possession of the necessary qualifications and credentials related to the job are usually important. Continuous learning and staying updated on industry trends and best practices are critical.

Experience and Competence
Proven experience and demonstrated competence in the relevant field are generally required. The ability to apply theoretical knowledge to real-world situations is a foundational requirement.

Adaptability and Flexibility
A willingness and an ability to adapt to changing circumstances and evolving organisational needs are critical. Flexibility in handling diverse tasks and responsibilities is also crucial.

Strong Work Ethic
A commitment to high standards of professionalism and ethical conduct is essential. Consistent dedication to achieving goals and meeting deadlines is mandatory.

Effective Communication Skills
Clear and concise verbal and written communication skills will be evident. The ability to convey information in a manner that is easily understood by others is readily demonstrated.

Teamwork and Collaboration
The capacity to work effectively in a team and collaborate with colleagues is mandatory. The contribution to a positive and supportive team culture will be consistent.

Problem-Solving Skills
Strong analytical and problem-solving abilities are demonstrated. The capacity to approach challenges with creativity and a solution-oriented mindset will be on display.

Leadership Qualities
Leadership skills, whether in a formal leadership role or through informal influence, are developed, supported, and valued. Opportunities will be provided to enhance the ability to inspire and motivate others toward common goals.

Interpersonal Skills
Effective interpersonal skills, including empathy and the ability to build positive relationships, are compulsory. Respectful and inclusive interactions with colleagues and stakeholders are mandatory.

Initiative and Proactivity
Willingness to take initiative and proactively identify and address issues will be promoted. The capacity to go above and beyond basic job requirements to contribute to organisational success is a mandatory requirement.

Time Management
Strong organisational and time management skills must be evident. This will be demonstrated by prioritising tasks and managing workload effectively.

Adherence to Policies and Procedures
A commitment to following organisational policies and procedures is required. This will be evident by consistent compliance with relevant regulations and standards.

Continuous Improvement Mindset
There is a commitment to personal and professional development. Personnel will demonstrate this by their willingness to learn from experiences and actively seek opportunities for improvement.

Customer Focus
There is a focus on understanding and meeting the needs of internal and external customers. All personnel are responsive and attentive to feedback.

Cultural Competence and Diversity Awareness
An awareness and appreciation of cultural diversity are evident. Personnel have the ability to work effectively with individuals from various backgrounds.

Emotional Intelligence
Personnel display high emotional intelligence, including self-awareness and empathy. The ability to navigate and manage emotions effectively in the workplace is evident.

Tech Savviness
Personnel demonstrate competence in utilising relevant technologies and tools. Adaptability to new technologies and a willingness to learn are evident.

Resilience and Stress Management
Resilience in the face of challenges and effective stress management are critical requirements. Personnel demonstrate an awareness of personal wellbeing and the importance of work-life balance.

By emphasising these essential requirements, schools and organisations can build a highly effective and motivated workforce that contributes to the organisation's overall success and positive culture. Regular professional development, training, and feedback mechanisms are essential to support personnel in meeting these requirements and continuously improving their performance.

29
Conflict

What almost everyone dislikes are conflicts. I say almost everyone, as I have met people who seem to thrive in it!

Schools are prone to conflicts at all levels due to the diverse nature of any school. The worse part of a conflict is that it can spoil the day or days for the persons involved. For example, a student facing a school suspension will involve investigations that may take two days or more to complete, followed by meetings with parents, support, and senior staff before a determination is made. Add the record-keeping and a full week has passed with little other time for other important matters. This time for those involved creates a great deal of stress and angst.

However, the goal for all principals will be to resolve all (or as many as possible) conflicts by providing solutions that will work. Yet, there may be conflicts when the best resolution may be for the family to find another school because the current school cannot meet or satisfy the student's needs.

Let's look at some of the conflicts arising at each stakeholder level.

Student Conflicts
Student conflicts at school may involve bullying (cyber, teasing, body shaming, etc.), friendships, home issues, plagiarism, teacher-student relationships, learning, wellbeing, and behaviour. These are all time-consuming issues and, unfortunately, there are not enough counsellors at school to support a significant number of students, let alone all of them. In primary school, the teacher can be the best person to resolve a conflict as they usually know

the student best. Depending on their experience, they may need the support of members from the learning support team or senior management.

Parental Conflicts

Parental conflicts will often voice all the student conflicts mentioned above. But we must also add homework, sports, classroom management, and teacher behaviour. It will demonstrate a positive school ethos if all conflicts are resolved at the grassroots level. However, senior management support is often required for those irate parents who enter the school gates.

Staff Conflicts

Staff conflicts may arise from responsibilities and deadlines, such as duty supervision and student reporting. There may be union conflicts as well as performance concerns.

Performance and teacher behaviour conflicts are draining, especially when improvement targets are unmet.

Leadership Conflicts

Leadership conflicts will often relate to leadership ability (and experience). Poor planning, communication, decision-making, and resourcing often result in low staff morale. Disenfranchised staff will soon choose to find greener pastures or add disharmony to the low staff morale.

School Authority Conflicts

School authority conflicts relate to head office interference regarding funding, personnel, facilities, and resources. The usual frustration is the lack of local knowledge or, more often, the lack of adequate resourcing to resolve the conflict. These are troublesome conflicts because school authorities usually hold the power balance.

When facing and trying to resolve conflicts, there are a few key priorities:

- Understand the conflict by allowing the complainant time to articulate the concerns (and let off all steam) because knowing you are listening means you care, so they are ready to support you.
- Avoid a bureaucratic response (we'll look into it and let you know) or support an action that is clearly at odds with school policy and best practice (hitting a student).
- Suggest actions and a timeline so that the complainant appreciates you are taking the matter seriously.
- Act immediately after the meeting and see how quickly the conflict can be resolved.

Ensure an open and transparent school climate in which all stakeholders understand their role and how important it is for everyone to always act in the best interests of the students.

30
Development

Development is a fundamental requirement for successful schools and organisations for several reasons, as it contributes to organisational growth, adaptability, employee satisfaction, and overall effectiveness. Here are key reasons why development is crucial for organisational success.

Adaptation to Change
The business environment is dynamic, with technological changes, market conditions, and customer expectations. Development enables organisations to adapt to these changes, ensuring they remain relevant and competitive.

Innovation and Creativity
Continuous development fosters a culture of innovation and creativity. Employees who are encouraged to develop their skills are more likely to contribute fresh ideas and solutions to organisational challenges.

Employee Engagement and Satisfaction
Investing in the development of employees demonstrates a commitment to their professional growth. This, in turn, enhances employee engagement and satisfaction, leading to higher morale and retention rates.

Increased Productivity
Well-developed employees are more likely to be proficient in their roles, increasing productivity. Development programs can improve efficiency, streamline processes, and enhance organisational performance.

Talent Retention
Employees are likelier to stay with an organisation that invests in their development. Development opportunities contribute to a positive workplace culture and demonstrate that the organisation values its workforce.

Leadership Development
Leadership is critical for organisational success. Development programs identify and nurture future leaders, ensuring a strong leadership pipeline that can guide the organisation through challenges and changes.

Enhanced Skills and Competencies
The business landscape is becoming increasingly complex. Development programs equip employees with the skills and competencies to excel in their current roles and take on new challenges.

Better Decision-Making
Well-developed individuals possess a broader knowledge base and critical thinking skills. This leads to better decision-making at all levels of the organisation, contributing to strategic success.

Increased Adaptability and Flexibility
Development encourages a learning mindset, making employees more adaptable and flexible. This is crucial in an environment where organisations must respond quickly to changes and uncertainties.

Competitive Advantage
Organisations that prioritise development gain a competitive advantage. A skilled and adaptable workforce can differentiate the organisation from competitors, attracting customers and top talent.

Succession Planning
Development initiatives contribute to effective succession planning. Identifying and developing employees for future leadership roles ensures a smooth transition in key positions, preventing leadership gaps.

Employee Morale and Motivation
Knowing that their organisation invests in their development boosts employee morale and motivation. This positive atmosphere contributes to a more engaged and productive workforce.

Organisational Resilience
Well-developed organisations are better equipped to navigate challenges and uncertainties. Development fosters resilience by preparing individuals and teams to overcome obstacles and adapt to changing circumstances.

Customer Satisfaction
Development programs that focus on customer service skills contribute to improved customer satisfaction. Employees trained to understand and meet customer needs can enhance the customer experience.

Strategic Growth
Development is essential for organisations that aim for strategic growth. As employees acquire new skills and knowledge, the organisation can expand into new markets, offer new products/ services, and pursue diverse opportunities.

In summary, development is fundamental for successful organisations because it empowers individuals, enhances organisational capabilities, and positions the business for sustained growth and competitiveness in a dynamic and ever-evolving environment.

While the fundamental principles of organisational development apply broadly, some unique aspects and variations exist when considering schools as organisations. Here are key points that highlight the specific characteristics and considerations for school organisational development.

Education Mission and Values
Schools have a distinct mission focused on education, learning, and the development of students. Organisational development in schools aligns closely with these educational goals and values.

Student-Centric Focus
The primary stakeholders in schools are students. Organisational development efforts often centre around enhancing teaching and learning experiences to meet the diverse needs of students.

Curriculum and Teaching Development
School development includes ongoing efforts to improve curriculum design, teaching methodologies, and assessment strategies. Schools strive to provide high-quality and relevant educational experiences for students.

Professional Development for Educators
Professional development is critical for teachers and staff. School organisational development strongly emphasises continuous learning, skill enhancement, and staying abreast of educational best practices.

Student Support Services
Schools often integrate organisational development efforts to enhance student support services, including counselling, special education, and academic and social-emotional growth interventions.

Parent and Community Engagement
Successful school organisational development includes strategies to engage parents and the local community. Building strong

partnerships with parents and community members is essential for the school's overall success.

Safety and Wellbeing
Safety protocols and wellbeing initiatives are integral to school organisational development. Schools prioritise creating a secure and supportive environment for both students and staff.

School Culture and Climate
The development of a positive school culture is a key focus. Promoting inclusivity, respect, and a sense of belonging contribute to a healthy and supportive school climate.

Data-Driven Decision Making
Schools use data to inform decision-making, not only in terms of student performance but also for improving instructional strategies, identifying growth areas, and evaluating school programs' effectiveness.

School Governance
The organisational structure in schools includes a unique governance structure involving administrators, teachers, parents, and sometimes students. Decision-making processes often involve collaborative efforts to ensure the school's success.

Unique Regulatory Environment
Schools operate within a unique regulatory environment with specific requirements related to education standards, student assessments, and compliance with local, state, and national educational policies.

Continuous Improvement and Accreditation
Many schools undergo accreditation processes that emphasise continuous improvement. Organisational development in schools is often aligned with accreditation standards and goals for improvement.

Student Leadership and Engagement
Schools may incorporate strategies to develop student leadership skills and actively involve students in decision-making, fostering a sense of responsibility and ownership in the school community.

Extracurricular and Co-Curricular Programs
School organisational development extends to extracurricular and co-curricular programs, aiming to provide a well-rounded educational experience beyond the classroom.

While the overarching principles of organisational development apply universally, the specific focus areas and priorities in schools are tailored to the unique mission and characteristics of educational institutions. The ultimate goal is to create a conducive and effective learning environment that maximises the potential for student success and wellbeing.

SECTION 5

COMMUNICATION

Good communication is like oil in a machine. It keeps everything running smoothly. Be wary of distorted messages, assumptions and misunderstandings, lack of feedback, and time constraints, as these are constant issues to effective communication.
— *Ken Darvall*

31
Who

In the context of communication during organisational change, many key players have crucial roles in facilitating effective communication and managing the change process.

Senior Leaders/Executives
Senior leaders and executives drive the change and set the overall vision and strategy. They are crucial in communicating the rationale behind the change, its benefits, and the organisation's commitment to its success.

Change Management Team
A dedicated change management team is often formed to plan, execute, and monitor the change initiative. This team is responsible for developing communication strategies, addressing resistance, and ensuring the change aligns with the organisation's goals.

Middle Managers
Middle managers act as a bridge between senior leadership and front-line employees. They play a pivotal role in translating the change message into actionable steps for their teams. Middle managers are often key communicators and influencers during the change process.

Front-Line Employees
The change directly impacts front-line employees. Their understanding, buy-in, and active participation are critical for successfully implementing the change. Effective communication ensures that they are informed about the changes and understand their role in the process.

Communication Specialists
Communication specialists or internal communication teams are responsible for crafting and delivering consistent messages across various channels. They work closely with leadership to ensure clear communication is timely and tailored to different audiences.

Training and Development Specialists
Specialists in training and development play a key role in preparing employees for the changes. They design and deliver training programs to equip employees with the skills and knowledge to adapt to new processes and technologies.

Employee Representatives or Unions
In organisations where unions or other representative bodies represent employees, these entities become key players. Engaging with employee representatives early in the process helps address concerns and gain their support.

External Consultants
Organisations often bring in external consultants with expertise in change management to provide insights, guidance, and additional resources. Consultants can offer a fresh perspective and support the internal teams in managing the change effectively.

Legal and Compliance Experts
Change initiatives may have legal and compliance implications. Legal and compliance experts ensure that the organisation adheres to relevant laws and regulations throughout the change process.

Customers and Clients
For some organisations, especially those in service industries, customers and clients are important stakeholders. Communication strategies may include keeping customers informed about changes impacting them and addressing any concerns.

Suppliers and Partners

External partners, suppliers, and collaborators may also be affected by organisational changes. Communication with these stakeholders is essential to maintain strong relationships and ensure a smooth transition.

Effective communication during organisational change requires collaboration among these key players. Transparent and consistent messaging, active engagement, and a focus on addressing concerns contribute to a more successful change initiative. Regular feedback loops and adjustments to communication strategies based on the evolving needs of stakeholders are also essential for success.

32
What

Communicating effectively during organisational change requires careful consideration of the key messages that must be conveyed to various stakeholders. The messages should be clear and consistent and address the concerns and interests of different audiences. Here are several key messages to communicate during organisational change.

Rationale for Change
Clearly articulate the reasons behind the change. Explain the business drivers, challenges, or opportunities that necessitate the organisational change. Help stakeholders understand the need for the change and its connection to the overall vision and strategy.

Vision for the Future
Communicate a compelling vision of what the school or organisation will look like after implementing the change. Highlight the positive outcomes, benefits, and opportunities the change will bring. Help stakeholders see the bigger picture and the long-term goals.

Benefits to Stakeholders
Clearly outline the change's benefits for various stakeholders, including employees, customers, and the school or organisation. Address the "What's In It For Me" (WIIFM) for employees to gain support and commitment.

Impact on Jobs and Roles
Provide transparent information about how the change will impact different organisational roles. Address any changes in job responsibilities, reporting structures, or job functions. Offer support and resources for staff who may be affected.

Timelines
Communicate the timeline for the change, including key milestones and deadlines. Provide a roadmap that helps stakeholders understand the sequence of events and when they can expect to see and experience specific changes.

Opportunities for Input and Feedback
Emphasise that the organisation values input and feedback. Communicate mechanisms for stakeholders to share their thoughts, concerns, and ideas throughout the change process. This fosters a sense of inclusion and participation.

Support and Resources
Communicate the support and resources available to stakeholders during the change. This may include training programs, mentoring, counselling services, and other assistance needed to help stakeholders navigate the transition.

Change in Processes and Procedures
Communicate changes in processes, procedures, and workflows. Provide training and documentation to help employees understand and adapt to new working methods. Address any concerns related to the impact on daily tasks.

Leadership Commitment
Reinforce the commitment of leadership to the success of the change. Highlight the role of leaders in guiding the organisation through the transition and their availability to address questions and concerns.

Recognition of Employee Contributions
Acknowledge and recognise the contributions of employees to the organisation's success. Emphasise that the change is not a reflection of past shortcomings but a strategic move to position the organisation for future success.

Consistent Communication Channels
Clearly communicate the channels through which information will be shared. Whether it's through town hall meetings, emails, intranet updates, or other means, ensure consistency in messaging across various communication channels.

Celebration of Successes
Communicate and celebrate milestones and successes achieved during the change process. Recognise and appreciate the efforts of individuals and teams, reinforcing a positive and achievement-oriented culture.

Addressing Uncertainties and Concerns
Proactively address uncertainties and concerns that employees may have. Be transparent about what is known and what is still uncertain. Communicate plans for addressing and mitigating potential challenges.

Continuous Updates and Transparency
Commit to providing regular and transparent updates throughout the change process. Frequent communication helps build trust, reduces uncertainty, and informs employees about progress.

Cultural Values and Alignment
Reinforce the change's alignment with the organisation's values. Communicate how the change supports the organisation's cultural aspirations and contributes to a positive work environment.

Tailoring these critical messages to the specific context of the organisational change and the needs of different stakeholder groups is essential. Effective communication involves what is communicated and how the messages are delivered and received. Throughout the change process, it's essential to be adaptable, responsive, and attentive to the organisation's evolving needs and its people.

33
How

The effectiveness of communication during organisational change is not only determined by the content of the messages but also by the delivery methods chosen. The goal is to reach and engage diverse stakeholders through channels that suit their preferences and needs. There are various ways communication can be best delivered during organisational change.

Face-to-Face Communication
Town Hall Meetings: Gather stakeholders for town hall meetings where leaders can communicate key messages, address questions, and demonstrate transparency.

Face-to-Face Q&A Sessions: Host question-and-answer sessions with leaders to provide a forum for direct interaction and clarification.

Written Communication
Email Updates: Send email updates regularly to keep employees informed about changes, milestones, and other important developments.

Intranet Announcements: Use the school's intranet to post detailed information, FAQs, and resources related to the change.

Newsletters: Create newsletters that highlight success stories, recognise achievements, and share information about the change.

Visual Communication
Infographics: Use visual aids, such as infographics, charts, and diagrams, to simplify complex information and make it more digestible.

Videos: Create informational videos featuring leaders explaining the change, its benefits, and the vision for the future.

Interactive Communication
Webinars and Virtual Meetings: Conduct webinars or virtual meetings to reach remote or dispersed teams, allowing for interactive participation and engagement.

Interactive Workshops: Facilitate workshops encouraging participation, feedback, and collaboration among employees.

Leadership Communication
Leadership Messages: Have leaders share messages through various channels, reinforcing key messages and emphasising their commitment to the change.

Leadership Blogs: Establish leadership blogs or vlogs where leaders can share insights, updates, and perspectives in a more personal format.

Employee Forums and Focus Groups
Feedback Sessions: Organise focus groups or feedback sessions to allow employees to express their concerns, ask questions, and share feedback.

Employee Forums: Establish forums or discussion boards where employees can converse and share their thoughts about the change.

Training and Development Programs
Training Sessions: Conduct training sessions to equip employees with the skills and knowledge needed to adapt to new processes or technologies.

Online Learning Platforms: Utilise online platforms for e-learning modules, making training resources accessible to employees at their convenience.

Social Media Engagement
Social Media Platforms: Leverage social media platforms to share updates and success stories and engage employees more informally and interactively.

Yammer or Workplace Platforms: Use enterprise social networking platforms for real-time communication, collaboration, and discussions.

Pilot Programs and Testimonials
Pilot Programs: Implement small-scale pilot programs to test changes before full implementation, gather feedback, and adjust.

Employee Testimonials: Share success stories and testimonials from employees who have embraced the change, providing positive examples for others.

Surveys
Use surveys to gather feedback, assess communication efforts' effectiveness, and identify areas for improvement.

Coaching and Mentoring
Coaching Sessions: Offer coaching sessions to support employees in navigating the change, addressing concerns, and building resilience.

Mentoring Programs: Establish mentoring programs where experienced employees can guide and support those adapting to change.

Branding and Symbolism
Change Branding: Create a recognisable brand or visual identity for the change initiative, reinforcing messages and building a sense of unity.

Symbolic Gestures: Introduce symbolic gestures or events representing the change, creating a shared experience for employees.

Mobile Apps
Develop or use mobile apps to deliver push notifications, updates, and resources directly to employees' mobile devices.

Printed Materials
Distribute printed materials, such as brochures and posters, to provide tangible information about the change.

Ongoing Feedback Mechanisms
Establish ongoing feedback channels, such as suggestion boxes, to encourage continuous employee input.

Choosing the right combination of these communication methods depends on the organisation's culture, the preferences of its employees, and the nature of the change. A multi-channel approach that combines various methods can enhance the reach and impact of communication efforts, ensuring that messages are accessible, relevant, and effectively received by diverse stakeholders.

34
When

Communication timing during organisational change is crucial to manage expectations, minimise uncertainty, and facilitate a smooth transition. Communication should occur at various stages of the change process to keep stakeholders informed and engaged. Here are key points to consider when communication should occur during organisational change.

Pre-Announcement Preparation
Prepare for the change by ensuring leaders and communication teams understand the details clearly. Develop key messages, anticipate potential questions, and establish communication channels.

Announcement Phase
Once leaders and communication teams are ready, formally announce the change to stakeholders. This should include the rationale for the change, the vision for the future, and initial details about the change process.

Immediate Follow-Up
Immediately following the announcement, schedule Q&A sessions, town hall meetings, or other forums for employees to ask questions and seek clarifications. This helps address immediate concerns and provides an opportunity for direct communication.

Throughout the Change Planning Phase
Provide regular updates as the change is planned and details are solidified. Communicate key milestones, timelines, and any adjustments to the initial plan. This helps employees stay informed about the progress of the change initiative.

Training and Preparation Phase
Before implementing changes in processes or procedures, communicate the training and development programs available to employees. Highlight the resources and support provided to help them adapt to the new requirements.

Implementation Phase
During the implementation phase, provide real-time updates about progress, any unexpected issues, and how these issues are being addressed. Timely communication is crucial to managing expectations and addressing concerns.

Post-Implementation Review
After the change has been implemented, conduct a post-implementation review. Communicate the outcomes, successes, and lessons learned. Gather feedback from employees to understand their experiences and areas for improvement.

Ongoing Communication
Even after the initial phases of the change, maintain ongoing communication to reinforce the new ways of working, celebrate successes, and address any lingering concerns. Regular updates help embed the change into the organisational culture.

Celebration of Successes
Periodically share success stories related to the change. Highlight individual and team achievements, showcasing positive outcomes and reinforcing the benefits of the change.

Adaptation and Evolution
If adjustments or refinements to the change strategy are needed, communicate these changes promptly. Explain the reasons behind the adjustments and how they align with the overall goals of the change initiative.

Closure and Acknowledgement
When the change has been fully implemented, communicate a sense of closure. Acknowledge the efforts of individuals and teams throughout the change process, expressing gratitude for their contributions.

Reflection and Learning
Encourage a culture of reflection and learning from the change experience. Communicate the lessons learned, both in terms of successes and challenges, to inform future change initiatives.

Feedback Loops
Establish and maintain continuous feedback mechanisms throughout the change process. Act on feedback promptly to address concerns and improve communication strategies.

Proactive Communication During Uncertainties
If there are periods of uncertainty or unexpected challenges, communicate proactively. Address concerns, share information about the steps being taken, and provide reassurance about the organisation's commitment to managing the situation.

Employee Transitions and Onboarding
If the change involves organisational restructuring or personnel transitions, communicate details about the changes in roles, responsibilities, and reporting structures. Provide support for employees undergoing transitions.

Organisations can create well-informed and engaged stakeholders by incorporating communication at each stage of the change process. Consistent, transparent, and timely communication builds trust, reduces resistance, and contributes to the overall success of the organisational change initiative.

35
Why

Effective communication is critical in various aspects of organisational functioning and is fundamental to the success of any initiative, including organisational change. Here are several reasons why effective communication is crucial.

Clarity of Direction
Effective communication ensures all stakeholders understand the vision, goals, and objectives. This clarity of direction is essential for aligning individual efforts with organisational priorities.

Employee Engagement
Clear and transparent communication fosters employee engagement. When staff is well-informed about the organisation's goals, strategies, and changes, they are more likely to feel connected and motivated to contribute to its success.

Building Trust
Trust is the foundation of a healthy organisational culture. Effective communication builds trust by providing accurate information, being transparent about decision-making, and demonstrating consistent messaging.

Reducing Uncertainty
Change, by its nature, introduces uncertainty. Effective communication helps reduce uncertainty by providing information about the reasons for change, the expected outcomes, and the steps involved. This reduces anxiety and resistance among employees.

Conflict Resolution
Miscommunication can lead to misunderstandings and conflicts. Effective communication helps identify and address issues promptly, preventing misunderstandings from escalating into serious conflicts.

Enhancing Collaboration
Open and clear communication fosters collaboration among teams and individuals. When information flows freely, teams can work more cohesively, share ideas, and collaborate on projects effectively.

Improved Decision-Making
Effective communication ensures that relevant information is shared with decision-makers. This, in turn, improves the quality of decision-making as leaders have a comprehensive understanding of the situation and various perspectives.

Customer Relations
Communication with customers is vital for maintaining positive relationships. Clear and timely communication about products, services, and any changes can enhance customer satisfaction and loyalty.

Adaptability to Change
In times of change, effective communication is crucial. It helps employees understand the need for change, how it will impact them, and what is expected. This understanding is essential for successful change implementation.

Innovation and Creativity
A culture of effective communication encourages the sharing of ideas and feedback. This, in turn, supports innovation and creativity as employees feel empowered to contribute their insights without fear of miscommunication.

Employee Morale
Employees who feel well-informed and heard through effective communication are likelier to have higher morale. Positive morale contributes to a healthier work environment and increased productivity.

Efficient Problem-Solving
When communication channels are open, problems can be identified and addressed more efficiently. Teams can collaborate to find solutions and resolve issues before they escalate.

Compliance and Alignment
Effective communication helps ensure that employees are aware of organisational policies, procedures, and expectations. This alignment promotes compliance with standards and contributes to a cohesive organisational culture.

Time and Resource Efficiency
Clear communication reduces the likelihood of misunderstandings and the need for repeated clarification. This saves time and resources that might otherwise be spent rectifying communication-related issues.

Organisational Reputation
External communication influences its reputation, including how an organisation communicates with the public and stakeholders. Effective communication can enhance the organisation's image and credibility.

In summary, effective communication is a cornerstone of organisational success. It facilitates understanding, collaboration, and adaptability, contributing to a positive and productive organisational culture. Whether in day-to-day operations or during times of change, clear and transparent communication is a key driver of organisational effectiveness.

36
Articulation

Articulation is crucial in communicating messages effectively, especially during organisational change. The way messages are expressed, the choice of words, and the clarity of communication impact how well the audience understands, accepts, and embraces the information. Here are several reasons why articulation is important in the communication of organisational messages.

Clarity of Information
Articulate communication ensures that messages are clear and easily understood. Ambiguity and vague language can lead to misunderstandings, confusion, and misinterpreting important information.

Building Understanding
Articulate communication helps build a shared understanding among all stakeholders. When messages are expressed clearly and precisely, individuals are more likely to grasp the intended meaning and align their understanding with organisational goals.

Minimising Misinterpretations
Miscommunication often stems from unclear or poorly articulated messages. Articulate communication minimises the risk of misinterpretation, reducing the likelihood of rumours, misinformation, and the spread of inaccurate details.

Gaining Buy-In and Support
Well-articulated messages are more persuasive. When leaders express their ideas, vision, and rationale for change in a compelling and articulate manner, they are more likely to gain buy-in and support from employees and other stakeholders.

Fostering Trust
Clear and articulate communication fosters trust. When individuals can rely on the accuracy and consistency of messages, they are more likely to trust the information being shared by leaders and the organisation as a whole.

Managing Expectations
Articulate communication is essential for managing expectations. Leaders need to communicate what stakeholders can expect during the change process, addressing both positive outcomes and potential challenges.

Addressing Concerns Proactively
Articulate communication allows leaders to address concerns and questions that may arise proactively. Leaders can incorporate clear explanations into their messages by anticipating potential points of confusion or resistance.

Motivating and Inspiring
Articulate communication is motivational. Inspirational messages that are well-articulated can inspire and motivate employees, creating a sense of purpose and commitment to the organisational vision.

Empowering Employees
Articulate communication empowers employees by providing them with the information they need to make informed decisions. When employees are well-informed, they feel empowered to contribute ideas, ask questions, and actively participate in the change process.

Creating a Positive Tone
The tone of communication matters. Well-articulated messages can convey an optimistic tone, even during challenging times. This positivity contributes to a more resilient and adaptive organisational culture.

Alignment with Organisational Values
Articulate communication ensures that messages align with the organisation's values. Messages consistent with organisational principles and values enhance credibility and reinforce the organisation's identity.

Encouraging Feedback
Clear articulation encourages open and constructive feedback. When individuals understand the message, they are more likely to provide meaningful input, leading to continuous improvement and refinement of communication strategies.

Adaptability to Different Audiences
Different stakeholders may have varying levels of expertise and different communication preferences. Articulate communication allows leaders to adapt their messages to different audiences, ensuring that the information is accessible and relevant to all.

Navigating Complexity
During complex changes, articulate communication is essential. Leaders need to break down complex concepts into digestible and understandable messages, helping employees navigate the intricacies of the change initiative.

Reinforcing Accountability
Articulate communication reinforces accountability. Clearly expressed expectations and responsibilities help individuals understand their roles, fostering a sense of accountability and ownership in the change process.

In summary, the importance of articulation in communication must be considered. It is a key element in conveying messages effectively, promoting understanding, and facilitating positive responses from stakeholders. Leaders who prioritise articulate communication contribute to a culture of clarity, trust, and collaboration within the school or organisation.

SECTION 6

PROJECTS

Successful projects, like the legendary holy grail, are highly sought after because they achieve goals, boost morale, enhance reputation, and provide learning.
— *Ken Darvall*

37
Need

Determining the need for an organisational change project is a critical decision that should be carefully considered. Several key considerations should be considered to assess whether a change initiative is necessary. Here are some important considerations:

Business Strategy Alignment
Evaluate whether the proposed change aligns with the overall strategic objectives of the school or organisation. The change should contribute to achieving the business strategy and long-term goals.

Market and Industry Changes
Consider external factors such as market trends, technological advancements, regulatory changes, and industry shifts. Schools and organisations need to adapt to changes in the external environment to remain competitive.

Performance Gaps
Assess the organisation's current performance against established benchmarks and goals. Identify areas where there are significant gaps or opportunities for improvement.

Customer and Stakeholder Expectations
Gather feedback from customers and key stakeholders. Consider whether the current organisational structure, processes, or offerings align with the expectations and needs of customers and stakeholders.

Employee Feedback and Engagement
Conduct employee surveys or engage in regular feedback sessions to understand employee perceptions. Low morale, high turnover, or resistance to current practices may indicate a need for change.

Technology and Innovation
Evaluate the organisation's current technology infrastructure and capabilities. Assess whether new technologies or innovations could enhance efficiency, productivity, and competitiveness.

Organisational Culture
Consider whether the current organisational culture supports the desired outcomes. If there is a misalignment between the existing culture and the desired changes, a change initiative may be needed to shift the culture.

Financial Performance
Analyse financial performance, including revenue, costs, and profitability. Identify financial indicators that suggest the need for organisational adjustments to improve financial health.

Risk Analysis
Assess potential risks and vulnerabilities in the current organisational structure and processes. Identify risks that may hinder the organisation's ability to achieve its objectives.

Legal and Regulatory Compliance
Evaluate whether the organisation complies with relevant laws and regulations. Changes may be necessary to ensure legal compliance and mitigate legal risks.

Competitive Landscape
Analyse the competitive landscape. If competitors are adopting new practices or gaining a competitive advantage, consider whether similar changes are necessary for the organisation to maintain or improve its market position.

Organisational Structure and Processes
Assess the efficiency and effectiveness of current organisational structures and processes. Identify bottlenecks, redundancies, or areas where improvements can be made.

Strategic Change Champions
Determine whether there is leadership support for the proposed change. Having committed leaders who champion the change is crucial for its success.

Capacity for Change
Assess the organisation's readiness for change. Consider factors such as the availability of resources, the capacity for change management, and the ability to adapt to new ways of working.

Learning from Past Initiatives
Reflect on the outcomes of previous change initiatives. Identify lessons learned and consider how past experiences can inform the planning and implementation of new changes.

Sustainability and Environmental Considerations
Consider whether changes are needed to align with sustainability goals or address environmental concerns. Organisations are increasingly incorporating sustainability into their strategies.

Global and Cultural Considerations
If the organisation operates in diverse cultural contexts, assess whether changes are needed to accommodate cultural differences and global requirements.

By thoroughly considering these factors, organisations can make informed decisions about the need for an organisational change project. Involving key stakeholders, including leadership, employees, and external partners, in the assessment process ensures a comprehensive understanding of the organisational landscape and challenges.

38
Initiative

Organisational change in schools is a complex process requiring careful planning, communication, and stakeholder collaboration. The initiatives for organisational change in schools should be aligned with the overarching goal of improving educational outcomes, enhancing the learning environment, and fostering the overall well-being of students and staff. Here are some appropriate initiatives for organisational change in schools.

Curriculum Redesign
Regularly review and update the curriculum to ensure it aligns with educational standards, addresses the needs of diverse learners, and incorporates innovative teaching methodologies.

Technology Integration
Integrate technology into the teaching and learning process. This may include providing devices for students, implementing online resources, and fostering digital literacy among teachers.

Professional Development Programs
Offer ongoing professional development opportunities for teachers to enhance their skills, stay updated on educational trends, and implement best practices in the classroom.

Student-Centred Approaches
Implement student-centred approaches such as project-based learning to foster critical thinking, collaboration, and problem-solving skills among students.

Inclusion Education Practices
Develop and implement inclusive education practices to create a supportive learning environment for students with diverse abilities and needs.

Assessment and Evaluation Reform
Explore alternative assessment methods beyond traditional testing, including project assessments, portfolios, and performance-based evaluations.

School Climate and Culture Improvement
Implement programs to improve school climate and culture, emphasising respect, inclusivity, and a positive learning environment for both students and staff.

Social Emotional Learning (SEL) Programs
Integrate social-emotional learning into the curriculum to support the emotional well-being of students and enhance their interpersonal skills.

Leadership Development
Provide leadership development programs for school administrators to enhance their skills in effective leadership, communication, and decision-making.

Data-Driven Decision Making
Encourage the use of data to inform decision-making processes. This includes analysing student performance data, attendance records, and other metrics to identify areas for improvement.

Flexible Learning Spaces
Explore flexible learning spaces that accommodate different teaching and learning styles, fostering creativity, collaboration, and adaptability.

Culturally Responsive Teaching
Provide educators with training on culturally responsive teaching practices to ensure that the curriculum reflects the diversity of the student population.

Environmental Sustainability Programs
Implement environmentally sustainable practices within the school, such as recycling programs, energy conservation, and eco-friendly initiatives.

Health and Wellness Initiatives
Implement programs that promote physical fitness, mental health awareness, and healthy lifestyle choices to prioritise the health and wellbeing of students and staff.

Student Voice and Leadership
Create opportunities for students to have a voice in decision-making processes and develop leadership skills through student government and other leadership programs.

Community Service and Civic Engagement
Integrate service-learning opportunities into the curriculum, allowing students to engage in community service and apply their learning to real-world situations.

Parent Education Programs
Offer workshops and programs for parents on effective parenting, supporting their child's education, and understanding the school curriculum.

It's important to note that successful organisational change in schools requires collaboration, ongoing communication, and a commitment to continuous improvement. Additionally, involving all stakeholders—including teachers, students, parents, administrators, and the community—ensures a holistic and sustainable approach to positive change in the educational environment.

39
Actions

Organisational change in schools involves a series of strategic actions to plan, implement, and sustain the desired transformation effectively. The following vital actions can guide the process of organisational change in schools.

Establish a Clear Vision
Develop a clear and compelling vision for the change. Clearly articulate the desired outcomes and benefits of the change initiative, ensuring alignment with the school's mission and goals.

Change Leadership Team
Form a dedicated change leadership team comprising representatives from various stakeholder groups, including administrators, teachers, parents, and community members. This team will play a crucial role in guiding the change process.

Communication and Stakeholder Engagement
Develop a comprehensive communication plan to keep all stakeholders informed about the change. Foster open and transparent communication channels and actively engage with teachers, students, parents, and the broader community.

Needs Assessment
Conduct a thorough needs assessment to identify areas that require change. Consider input from teachers, students, and parents to understand challenges and opportunities comprehensively.

Detailed Change Plan
Develop a detailed change plan outlining specific goals, milestones, timelines, and responsibilities. Break down the plan into manageable phases to facilitate effective implementation.

Professional Development
Offer targeted professional development opportunities for teachers and staff to enhance their skills and competencies related to the proposed changes. This ensures that educators are well-equipped to implement new strategies and methodologies.

Culture of Collaboration
Cultivate a collaborative culture where teachers, administrators, and staff work together toward common goals. Encourage collaboration through team-building activities, shared decision-making, and collaborative planning.

Staff Empowerment
Empower teachers and staff to be active participants in the change process. Provide opportunities for input, feedback, and decision-making, fostering a sense of ownership and commitment.

Address Resistance
Anticipate and address resistance to change. Identify potential sources of resistance and develop strategies to mitigate concerns. Communicate the benefits of the change and support those adapting to new practices.

Pilot Programs
Consider implementing pilot programs or small-scale initiatives to test the proposed changes in a controlled environment. Gather participant feedback to identify strengths and areas for improvement before full-scale implementation.

Monitoring
Establish a system for monitoring progress and evaluating the effectiveness of the change initiative. Use data and feedback to make necessary adjustments and ensure that the change meets its goals.

Celebrate
Acknowledge and celebrate milestones and successes throughout the change process. Recognise the efforts of teachers, students, and staff, reinforcing a positive and achievement-oriented culture.

Ongoing Support
Offer ongoing support for teachers and staff as they navigate the changes. This may include mentorship programs, additional training, and resources to ensure sustained success.

Evaluation and Reflection
Conduct a comprehensive evaluation of the change initiative once it has been fully implemented. Reflect on what worked well, areas for improvement, and lessons learned. Use this information to inform future change efforts.

Sustaining Change
Develop strategies for sustaining the positive changes over the long term. This may involve embedding new practices into the school culture, revising policies, and reinforcing the changes' importance.

Ongoing Communication
Maintain ongoing communication to keep stakeholders informed about the progress and outcomes of the change. Address any lingering questions or concerns and continue reinforcing the importance of the change initiative.

Professional Learning Communities
Establish Professional Learning Communities where teachers can collaborate, share best practices, and engage in continuous learning. This collaborative structure supports ongoing professional development and facilitates the exchange of ideas.

Flexibility and Adaptability
Foster a culture of flexibility and adaptability. Recognise that the educational landscape is dynamic, and schools need to be responsive to evolving needs. Encourage a mindset of continuous improvement.

By taking these key actions, schools can navigate the complexities of organisational change, effectively engage stakeholders, and create an environment that promotes positive outcomes for students and the entire school community. Successful organisational change in schools requires strategic planning, collaboration, and a commitment to ongoing improvement.

40
Experiences

Experiencing organisational change in schools can be multifaceted, involving various challenges and opportunities. Here are some key experiences that individuals—including teachers, administrators, students, and parents—may encounter during school organisational change.

Uncertainty and Ambiguity
Individuals may experience uncertainty and ambiguity about the changes, especially if the details of the change initiative are not clearly communicated. This uncertainty can lead to anxiety and apprehension.

Resistance to Change
Resistance is a common experience during organisational change. Some individuals may resist due to concerns about how it will impact their roles, routines, or the overall school environment.

Concerns About Impact on Students
Teachers and parents may express concerns about how the change will affect students. These concerns include the quality of education, student wellbeing, and the overall learning experience.

Increased Workload
Teachers and staff may experience an increased workload when implementing change initiatives, particularly if new processes or technologies require additional time and effort.

Professional Development Opportunities
Teachers may have the opportunity to engage in professional development to acquire new skills and knowledge related to the changes. This can be an empowering experience for educators.

Collaboration and Teamwork
The change process may encourage collaboration and teamwork among teachers, administrators, and staff. Working together to implement changes can foster a sense of shared responsibility.

Training and Support Programs
Schools may provide training and support programs to help individuals navigate the changes. This can include workshops, mentorship programs, and resources to facilitate a smooth transition.

Communication Challenges
Effective communication is crucial during organisational change, but communication challenges may arise. Miscommunication, lack of information, or unclear messaging can contribute to misunderstandings.

Celebration of Successes
Celebrating small and large successes during the change process can create a positive atmosphere and reinforce the benefits of the change. Recognition of achievements helps build momentum and morale.

Shift in School Culture
The change process may contribute to a shift in school culture. This could involve a greater emphasis on collaboration, innovation, or a focus on specific values aligned with the change initiative.

Student Involvement and Engagement
Students may participate in the change process through feedback sessions, student forums, or specific initiatives. Engaging students can foster a sense of ownership in the school environment.

Impact on Parental Involvement
Changes in school practices may impact parental involvement. Parents may need to adapt to new communication methods,

engagement strategies, or expectations for involvement in their child's education.

Evaluation and Reflection
The change process may involve ongoing evaluation and reflection. This could include periodic assessments of the effectiveness of the changes and opportunities for stakeholders to provide feedback.

Building a Learning Organisation
The change experience can contribute to the development of a learning organisation—a school that values continuous improvement, adapts to new challenges, and actively seeks growth opportunities.

Cultural Shifts
Organisational change can lead to cultural shifts within the school community. This may involve changes in norms, values, and the way individuals interact with one another.

Adaptive Leadership
Administrators may experience the need for adaptive leadership skills, including the ability to guide the organisation through change, respond to challenges, and foster a positive and resilient school culture.

Addressing Equity and Inclusion
Organisational change may provide opportunities to address issues of equity and inclusion within the school. This includes ensuring that the benefits of the change are accessible to all students and stakeholders.

Continuous Improvement Mindset
The change experience can instil a continuous improvement mindset within the school community, emphasising the importance of learning from experiences, adapting to feedback, and seeking opportunities for refinement.

It's important to recognise that experiences during organisational change can vary widely among individuals and groups. Effective leadership, clear communication, and a focus on collaboration can contribute to a more positive and successful school change experience.

41
Opportunities

School organisational change presents various opportunities for growth, improvement, and positive transformation. Recognising and capitalising on these opportunities can contribute to a successful change process. Here are key opportunities that may arise during organisational change in schools.

Innovative Teaching and Learning Practices
Organisational change can provide an opportunity to introduce and implement innovative teaching and learning practices. This may include integrating technology, project-based learning, and other student-centred approaches.

Professional Development and Skills Enhancement
Change initiatives often create opportunities for professional development. Teachers and staff can enhance their skills, acquire new knowledge, and stay current with best practices in education.

Enhanced Collaboration and Teamwork
Organisational change can foster a culture of collaboration and teamwork. Teachers, administrators, and staff may collaborate more closely, sharing ideas, resources, and responsibilities.

Focus on Student Wellbeing
Changes in organisational practices can provide an opportunity to prioritise and enhance student wellbeing. This may involve initiatives related to social-emotional learning, mental health support, and creating a positive school culture.

Community Engagement and Partnerships
Schools can use the change process to strengthen community engagement and build partnerships. Involving parents, local businesses, and community organisations can enrich the educational experience.

Equity and Inclusion Initiatives
Organisational change presents a chance to address issues of equity and inclusion within the school. Schools can implement initiatives to ensure equal access to resources, opportunities, and a supportive learning environment for all students.

Student Voice and Leadership Opportunities
Changes in school practices may create opportunities for students to have a more significant voice in decision-making processes. Student leadership programs and involvement in school governance can empower students.

Data-Informed Decision-Making
Change initiatives often encourage a shift toward data-informed decision-making. Schools can use data analytics to assess student performance, identify areas for improvement, and make informed decisions about educational practices.

Cultural Shifts Towards Continuous Improvement
Organisational change can instil a cultural shift toward continuous improvement. Schools may adopt a mindset that values learning from experiences, adapting to feedback, and seeking opportunities for ongoing refinement.

Positive School Culture
Change processes offer an opportunity to cultivate a positive school culture. Emphasising values such as respect, inclusivity, and collaboration can contribute to a supportive and thriving school community.

Leadership Development
Change initiatives provide opportunities for leadership development. Administrators and aspiring leaders may have the chance to take on new responsibilities, demonstrate leadership skills, and contribute to the success of the change process.

Environmental Sustainability Initiatives
Schools can use the change process to implement environmental sustainability initiatives. This may include adopting eco-friendly practices, incorporating environmental education, and promoting sustainability within the school community.

Flexible Learning Environment
Changes in organisational structures may allow for the creation of flexible learning environments. Schools can explore different classroom setups and technology integration to support diverse learning styles.

Parental Involvement and Education
Change initiatives can enhance parental involvement and education. Schools may provide opportunities for parents to participate in workshops, understand changes in educational practices, and actively engage in their child's education.

Global and Cultural Awareness
Organisational change can facilitate a greater focus on global and cultural awareness. Schools may integrate diverse perspectives into the curriculum, fostering an understanding of different cultures and global issues.

Balanced Assessment Practices
Change processes provide an opportunity to reassess and implement more balanced assessment practices. Schools can explore alternative assessment methods that align with modern educational philosophies.

Teacher Empowerment
Change initiatives can empower teachers by giving them a voice in decision-making, opportunities for professional growth, and a sense of ownership in the educational process.

Adaptive and Resilient School Community
Successfully navigating organisational change can contribute to developing an adaptive and resilient school community. This mindset positions the school to handle future challenges flexibly and positively.

By recognising and embracing these opportunities, schools can harness the potential for positive change, ultimately improving the educational experience for students, teachers, and the entire school community.

42
Evidence

Evaluating the success of organisational change in schools involves examining various types of evidence during and after the change process. The evidence can help assess the impact of the change initiatives on students, teachers, administrators, and the school community. Here are key types of evidence that may be evident during and after organisational change in schools.

During Organisational Change

Communication Records
Evidence of effective communication, including clear messages, regular updates, and two-way communication channels.

Participation Rates
Data on the level of participation in change-related activities, such as workshops, training sessions, and collaborative planning meetings.

Feedback and Surveys
Stakeholder responses are captured through surveys and feedback mechanisms, capturing perceptions, concerns, and suggestions related to the change.

Documentation of Planning
Written plans, strategies, and documentation related to the change initiative, including goals, timelines, and responsibilities.

Training Attendance and Progress
Records of attendance at training sessions and evidence of progress in acquiring new skills and knowledge among teachers and staff.

Pilot Program Outcomes
Data and feedback from any pilot programs or small-scale implementations indicating strengths, weaknesses, and areas for improvement.

Collaborative Initiatives
Evidence of increased collaboration and teamwork includes joint projects, shared resources, and collaborative decision-making.

Adaptive Leadership Practices
Observations and evidence of adaptive leadership practices showcasing the ability of leaders to navigate challenges and guide the organisation through change.

After Organisational Change

Student Performance Data
Academic and non-academic performance data, comparing student outcomes before and after the change, including standardised test scores, grades, and graduation rates.

Teacher and Staff Retention Rates
Data on teacher and staff retention rates indicate whether the change has positively influenced job satisfaction and employee retention.

Student and Teacher Surveys
Continued feedback from students and teachers through surveys, assessing their experiences and perceptions after implementing the change.

Classroom Observations
Observations of classrooms to assess whether new teaching practices are being implemented effectively and whether they positively impact student engagement and learning.

Administrative Data
Administrative records related to attendance, disciplinary actions, and other relevant indicators, helping assess changes in school culture and student behaviour.

Innovative Learning Practices
There is evidence of the integration and success of innovative learning practices, such as technology integration, project-based learning, and other student-centred approaches.

Community Engagement Metrics
Data on community engagement and partnerships, measuring the involvement of parents, local businesses, and community organisations in school activities.

Sustainability of Changes
There must be evidence of the sustainability of changes over time, including whether the new practices have become embedded in the school culture and are consistently applied.

Equity and Inclusion
Indicators of progress in addressing issues of equity and inclusion, such as closing achievement gaps and creating an inclusive learning environment.

Financial Metrics
Financial data indicates whether the change has positively impacted the school's financial health and resource allocation.

Teacher Empowerment and Leadership
There is evidence of teacher empowerment and leadership, including examples of teachers taking on leadership roles, contributing to decision-making, and actively participating in professional development.

Positive School Culture
There are indicators of a positive school culture, such as increased morale, a sense of community, and positive interactions among students, teachers, and administrators.

Global and Cultural Awareness
Evidence of successfully integrating global and cultural awareness into the curriculum and school activities.

Continuous Improvement Initiatives
Evidence of a continuous improvement mindset, including ongoing evaluation, reflection, and adjustments based on feedback and outcomes.

Adaptive and Resilient School Community
Observations and evidence of an adaptive and resilient school community that can effectively navigate challenges and embrace change.

Collecting and analysing these types of evidence throughout the organisational change process provides a comprehensive understanding of the impact of the change initiatives and informs future decision-making and continuous improvement efforts within the school.

43
Celebrations

Celebrating an organisational change in schools is essential to recognising and reinforcing the positive outcomes of the change initiatives. Celebration serves multiple purposes, including acknowledging the efforts of stakeholders, fostering a positive school culture, and motivating individuals to continue embracing change. Here's how and why celebration is important after organisational change in schools.

How To Celebrate

Recognition Ceremonies
Conduct recognition ceremonies or events to acknowledge the contributions of individuals and teams who played a crucial role in the success of the change initiative. This could include teachers, administrators, support staff, and even actively participating students.

Showcase Success Stories
Share success stories and case studies that highlight positive outcomes resulting from the organisational change. This can be done through newsletters, school websites, or staff meetings to inspire and motivate others.

Express Gratitude
Express gratitude and appreciation openly. Leaders can personally thank individuals and teams for their dedication, hard work, and adaptability throughout the change process.

Create a Positive Atmosphere
Decorate common areas with positive messages, banners, or visuals that reflect the change initiative's success. Creating

a positive physical environment contributes to a celebratory atmosphere.

Celebrate Milestones
Celebrate specific milestones achieved during the change process. This could include reaching key objectives, successfully implementing new practices, or overcoming significant challenges.

Host Social Events
Organise social events or gatherings to bring the school community together in a relaxed and celebratory setting. This could be a picnic, or a themed celebration that fosters a sense of camaraderie.

Acknowledge Student Involvement
Acknowledge the students' role in the success of the change initiative. This can be done through student assemblies, recognition in newsletters, or showcasing student projects related to the changes.

Create Commemorative Items
Develop commemorative items such as certificates, plaques, or tokens of appreciation that can be presented to individuals or teams as a lasting reminder of their contribution to the change process.

Professional Development Opportunities
Offer professional development opportunities as a celebration. This could include workshops, seminars, or conferences that align with the skills and knowledge acquired during the change initiative.

Why Celebrate

Boost Morale and Motivation
Celebration boosts morale and motivation by recognising and validating the hard work and dedication of individuals and teams. It reinforces the idea that their efforts have made a positive impact.

Reinforce Positive Behaviours
Celebrating success reinforces positive behaviours and attitudes associated with the change. It encourages individuals to continue embracing new practices and approaches.

Build a Positive School Culture
Celebration builds a positive school culture by emphasising the importance of recognising achievements, collaboration, and a shared sense of accomplishment.

Create a Sense of Community
Celebratory events and activities create a sense of community within the school. This fosters connections among teachers, administrators, students, and parents, contributing to a supportive and united school environment.

Highlight the Value of Change
Celebration serves as a platform to highlight the value of change and its positive impact on the school community. It reinforces the notion that change is a positive force for improvement.

Encourage Reflection
The celebration provides an opportunity for reflection on the journey of organisational change. It allows stakeholders to look back on challenges overcome, lessons learned, and the growth achieved due to the change.

Inspire Confidence in Future Changes
By celebrating the success of one change initiative, the school community builds confidence in its ability to navigate and succeed in future changes. It establishes a culture that is open to innovation and improvement.

Acknowledge Collaboration
Celebrating emphasises the collaborative nature of the change process. It recognises that successful change requires many

efforts and reinforces the importance of working together toward common goals.

Improve Retention and Satisfaction
Recognising and celebrating achievements can improve staff retention and job satisfaction. Employees who feel valued and appreciated are likelier to be engaged and committed to the organisation.

Promote a Positive Narrative
Celebration helps create a positive narrative around the change initiative. This positive story can be shared with the wider community, fostering a positive reputation for the school and attracting support.

Cultivate a Culture of Continuous Improvement
Celebrating organisational change reinforces the idea that the school is on a journey of continuous improvement. It instils a mindset that embraces change as an ongoing process rather than a one-time event.

In summary, celebrating an organisational change in schools is a crucial step in recognising and reinforcing the positive impact of the change initiative. It creates a culture of appreciation, motivation, and shared accomplishment that contributes to the overall success and sustainability of the changes implemented.

SECTION 7

REPUTATION

A school or organisation's reputation is critical because it establishes trust and credibility, enables talent attraction and retention, can boost student enrolment numbers, and open doors for partnerships and collaboration. While building a reputation takes time, poor actions and decisions can damage a reputation in no time.

— *Ken Darvall*

44
Targets

When considering a school's reputation during organisational change, setting strategic targets is important to guide the process and measure success. Reputation is influenced by various factors, including academic performance, community engagement, and the perception of stakeholders. Here are some key targets to consider setting during organisational change to impact and enhance a school's reputation positively.

Academic Excellence
Academic excellence is a cornerstone of a school's reputation. Improving these metrics reflects positively on the school's commitment to quality education.

Target: Improve academic performance indicators, such as standardised test scores, graduation rates, and student achievement levels.

Student Satisfaction
Satisfied students are likely to speak positively about their school experience, contributing to a favourable perception of the school.

Target: Increase student satisfaction levels through surveys and feedback mechanisms.

Parental Involvement
Higher levels of parental engagement are often associated with a positive school environment and can contribute to a positive reputation within the community.

Target: Increase levels of parental involvement in school activities and events.

Community Partnerships
Positive collaborations with the community can enhance the school's reputation and demonstrate a commitment to community engagement.

Target: Establish or strengthen partnerships with local businesses, community organisations, and other stakeholders.

Communication Effectiveness
Effective communication fosters trust and keeps stakeholders informed, positively impacting the school's reputation.

Target: Improve communication effectiveness through clear, consistent, and transparent communication channels.

Positive Media Coverage
Positive media coverage can shape public perception and contribute to a positive narrative about the school.

Target: Generate positive media coverage by sharing success stories, achievements, and notable events.

Innovative Programs and Practices
Innovations in education can attract positive attention, showcasing the school as forward-thinking and committed to providing a modern and dynamic learning environment.

Target: Implement or enhance innovative educational programs and practices.

Staff Professional Development
A highly skilled and motivated teaching staff contributes to a positive reputation and enhances the overall quality of education.

Target: Increase staff participation in professional development opportunities.

Positive School Culture
A positive school culture contributes to a favourable reputation and can attract students, parents, and quality educators.

Target: Foster a positive school culture through initiatives that promote inclusivity, respect, and a sense of community.

Retention of High-Quality Staff
A stable and experienced staff positively influences the school's reputation and contributes to a consistent and high-quality educational experience.

Target: Retain high-quality teachers and staff.

Student Leadership and Achievement
Students' accomplishments and leadership roles positively affect the school's image and reputation.

Target: Encourage and celebrate student leadership opportunities and achievements.

Alumni Engagement
Positive relationships with alumni can lead to positive word-of-mouth endorsements and contribute to the school's reputation.

Target: Increase engagement with alumni through events, networks, and communication channels.

Recognition and Awards
External recognition enhances the school's reputation and can attract positive attention from the community and educational stakeholders.

Target: Strive for recognition and awards in educational excellence, community service, or other relevant categories.

Sustainability Initiatives
Commitment to sustainability reflects positively on the school's values and can contribute to a positive reputation.

Target: Implement or enhance sustainability initiatives within the school.

Positive Online Presence
Many stakeholders form their first impressions through online channels, so a positive and engaging online presence is crucial.

Target: Maintain and enhance a positive online presence through the school's website, social media, and other online platforms.

Effective Crisis Management
Responding effectively to challenges and crises can safeguard the school's reputation during difficult times.

Target: Develop and implement effective crisis management strategies.

Consistent Branding
A cohesive and positive brand image contributes to a strong and recognisable reputation.

Target: Ensure consistent and positive branding across all communication materials.

Survey Results and Benchmarks
Data-driven insights from surveys help track the impact of organisational change on the school's reputation.

Target: Set benchmarks for key reputation indicators and regularly conduct surveys to assess progress.

These targets should align with the school's mission, vision, and values. Regularly monitoring progress toward these targets and adjusting strategies as needed will contribute to a positive and sustainable enhancement of the school's reputation.

45
Timelines

Setting timelines during organisational change in schools is crucial for effective planning, implementation, and assessment of the impact on the school's reputation. The specific timelines can vary based on the nature and scope of the change initiative, but establishing clear milestones helps create a structured and measurable process. Here are key timelines to consider during organisational change in relation to managing and enhancing a school's reputation.

Pre-Implementation Phase

Planning and Needs Assessment
3-6 months
Conduct a thorough needs assessment to identify areas for improvement. Develop a comprehensive change plan outlining goals, strategies, and timelines. Establish a change leadership team and allocate responsibilities.

Communication Strategy Development
1-3 months
Develop a detailed communication strategy for internal and external stakeholders. Create messaging that emphasises the positive aspects of the upcoming changes.

Stakeholder Engagement
Ongoing
Engage with teachers, students, parents, and the community through feedback sessions.
Build awareness and garner support for the upcoming changes.

Implementation Phase

Pilot Programs and Small-Scale Implementation
6-12 months
Implement pilot programs to test the proposed changes in a controlled environment. Gather feedback and make adjustments based on pilot outcomes.

Communication Launch
At the start of implementation
Launch the communication plan, including announcements, newsletters, and informational sessions. Clearly communicate the goals and benefits of the changes to all stakeholders.

Training and Professional Development
Ongoing throughout implementation
Provide ongoing training and professional development opportunities for teachers and staff.
Ensure that educators are well-equipped to implement new practices.

Regular Progress Assessments
Quarterly
Assess progress against established benchmarks and milestones. Identify areas of success and address any challenges that arise.

Post-Implementation Phase

Evaluation and Reflection
6-12 months after full implementation
Conduct a comprehensive evaluation of the change initiative. Reflect on what worked well, areas for improvement, and lessons learned.

Celebration of Milestones
Throughout the post-implementation phase
Celebrate achievements and milestones reached during the change process. Acknowledge the efforts of individuals and teams.

Sustainability Planning
Ongoing
Develop strategies to sustain the positive changes over the long term. Integrate new practices into the school culture and policies.

Continued Communication
Ongoing
Maintain ongoing communication to keep stakeholders informed about progress. Address any lingering questions or concerns.

Surveys and Feedback
Annually
Conduct surveys and seek feedback from stakeholders to gauge satisfaction. Use data to make continuous improvements.

Adjustments and Iterations
Ongoing
Make adjustments to the organisational structure, policies, or practices as needed. Demonstrate responsiveness to feedback and changing circumstances.

Reassessing Reputation Metrics
Annually or as needed
Reassess reputation metrics, including surveys, media coverage, and community feedback.
Compare current reputation indicators with baseline data.

Strategic Planning for Future Initiatives
1-3 years
Begin strategic planning for future initiatives or improvements. Align future plans with the school's mission and ongoing commitment to excellence.

Continuous Improvement

Ongoing Monitoring and Reporting
Continuous
Establish a system for ongoing monitoring of key performance indicators. Regularly report progress to the school community and stakeholders.

Adaptation to Changing Needs
Continuous
Be prepared to adapt strategies and initiatives based on changing educational landscapes and community needs.

Crisis Preparedness and Management
Continuous
Ensure ongoing readiness for crisis management and communication. Regularly review and update crisis response plans.

Notes on Timelines
Timelines are flexible and may need adjustments based on the specific nature and scale of the change initiative. Communication should be ongoing and responsive, with regular updates provided to stakeholders. Celebrations and acknowledgments should be integrated throughout the process to maintain morale and motivation.

By setting these timelines, the school can ensure a structured and phased approach to organisational change, promoting transparency, engagement, and positive outcomes for the school's reputation.

46
Evidence

Evidence of a school's reputation during organisational change can be gathered from various sources and indicators. This evidence helps assess the impact of the change initiatives on the perception of stakeholders, including students, parents, teachers, and the broader community. Here are key types of evidence that should be available to evaluate a school's reputation during organisational change.

Stakeholders' Surveys and Feedback
Direct input from stakeholders provides valuable insights into their perceptions, satisfaction levels, and areas of concern or improvement.

Evidence: Results of surveys and feedback sessions from students, parents, teachers, and community members.

Media Coverage and Public Relations
Media coverage can influence public perception. Positive and balanced coverage can contribute to a favourable reputation.

Evidence: Analysis of media coverage, including news articles, press releases, and social media mentions.

Online Presence and Social Media Engagement
An active and positive online presence is crucial for shaping public perception, especially in the digital age.

Evidence: Metrics related to the school's online presence, including website analytics, social media engagement, and reviews.

Academic Performance Metrics
Academic success is a fundamental factor influencing a school's reputation.

Evidence: Academic performance indicators include standardised test scores, graduation rates, and college acceptance rates.

Student and Teacher Retention Rates
High retention rates indicate satisfaction and confidence in the school, contributing positively to its reputation.

Evidence: Data on student enrolment and retention rates, and teacher retention rates.

Community Engagement Metrics
Active community engagement fosters positive relationships and contributes to a favourable reputation.

Evidence: Data on community engagement, including attendance at school events, participation in parent-teacher meetings, and involvement in community programs.

Alumni Success Stories and Involvement
Positive alumni experiences can serve as powerful evidence of the school's impact and reputation.

Evidence: Examples of alumni success stories, testimonials, and the level of involvement of alumni in school activities.

Positive Testimonials and Endorsements
Authentic endorsements contribute to a positive narrative and demonstrate community support.

Evidence: Positive testimonials and endorsements from parents, students, and community members.

Innovative Programs and Practices
Innovation contributes to a positive reputation by showcasing the school's commitment to providing a modern and dynamic learning environment.

Evidence: Documentation of innovative educational programs, extracurricular activities, and teaching practices.

Community Partnerships and Collaborations
Collaborations and partnerships can enhance the school's reputation by showcasing its commitment to community engagement and providing diverse learning opportunities.

Evidence: Partnerships with businesses, community organisations, and educational institutions.

Enrolment Trends
An increase in enrolment or positive trends can indicate a favourable perception of the school and its programs among parents and students.

Evidence: Changes in student enrolment numbers and trends.

Surveys and Perception Studies
External assessments provide an unbiased view of the school's reputation and its standing within the broader educational community.

Evidence: Independent surveys or perception studies conducted by third-party organisations.

Notes on Evidence
Regularly collect, analyse, and update evidence to provide a comprehensive and current understanding of the school's reputation. Utilise a combination of qualitative and quantitative data to gain a holistic view of reputation-related factors. Ensure

that evidence aligns with the goals and values of the school and the objectives of the organisational change.

By collecting and analysing this evidence, school leaders can gain valuable insights into the impact of organisational change on the school's reputation and make informed decisions for ongoing improvement.

It's important to note that these pieces of evidence should be considered collectively, as a school's reputation is multifaceted and influenced by various factors. Regularly monitoring and assessing these indicators can help school leaders understand how organisational changes are perceived and make informed adjustments.

47
Impact

During organisational change in a school, several impacts on the school's reputation may be evident, depending on the nature of the changes and how they are managed. While each school's context is unique, positive and effective organisational change typically manifests in certain ways that contribute to an enhanced reputation. Here are some potential impacts that should be evident during organisational change.

Increased Stakeholder Satisfaction
A higher level of satisfaction indicates that the changes resonate positively with those directly affected by the school's programs and policies.

Impact: Positive changes should lead to increased satisfaction among key stakeholders, including students, parents, teachers, and the broader community.

Improved Academic Performance
Higher academic standards and outcomes contribute to a positive perception of the school's effectiveness and commitment to educational excellence.

Impact: Organisational changes that positively affect teaching and learning can improve academic performance and student achievement.

Enhanced School Culture and Climate
A supportive and inclusive school environment is attractive to students, parents, and educators, positively influencing the school's reputation.

Impact: Positive changes should contribute to a healthier and more positive school culture and climate.

Increased Community Engagement
A school that actively engages with its community demonstrates a commitment to collaboration and partnerships, which can enhance its reputation.

Impact: Successful organisational changes can result in increased community engagement, involvement, and support.

Effective Communication and Transparency
Clear and transparent communication fosters trust among stakeholders and helps manage expectations during times of change.

Impact: Open and transparent communication during organisational change can positively impact the school's reputation.

Recognition and Awards
External validation from educational bodies and recognition in awards contribute to a positive reputation.

Impact: Positive changes may lead to the school receiving recognition, awards, or accreditation.

Increased Teacher Satisfaction and Retention
A stable and satisfied teaching staff is often associated with effective leadership and a positive working environment, reflecting well on the school's reputation.

Impact: A positive impact on teacher satisfaction and retention rates.

Student and Alumni Success Stories
Stories of student achievement and success post-graduation contribute to the perception of the school as an institution that prepares students for future success.

Impact: Demonstrated success stories among current students and alumni.

Adaptation to 21st Century Learning
A school that embraces modern teaching methods and technology signals adaptability and relevance, positively influencing its reputation.

Impact: Successful integration of technology and 21st-century learning methods.

Positive Media Coverage
Favourable coverage in the media helps shape public perceptions and contributes to the overall positive image of the school.

Impact: Positive media coverage and public relations efforts.

Increased Enrolment and Retention
A growing or stable student population is often associated with a positive perception of the school's programs and offerings.

Evidence: Positive changes may result in increased enrolment and retention of students.

Demonstrated Fiscal Responsibility
Demonstrating fiscal responsibility contributes to the perception of the school as a well-managed institution, positively impacting its reputation.

Impact: Effective financial management and stewardship.

It's important to note that the impact on a school's reputation during organisational change is a dynamic and ongoing process. Schools should continuously assess the effectiveness of changes, solicit feedback from stakeholders, and make adjustments as needed to maintain or enhance their reputation within the educational community and the broader public.

48

Performance

The impact of organisational change on a school's reputation can be reflected in various performance indicators. These indicators provide evidence of how well the school is adapting to change and how it is perceived by stakeholders. Here are key performance indicators that may offer evidence of a school's reputation during organisational change.

Academic Performance
Positive changes in academic outcomes indicate that the organisational changes are positively influencing teaching and learning.

Evidence: Improved student achievement, higher standardised test scores, and positive trends in academic performance.

Graduation Rates
Higher graduation rates suggest that students are successfully completing their education, contributing positively to the school's reputation.

Evidence: Increased graduation rates and a reduction in dropout rates.

Student Success in Post-Secondary Education
Students' success in pursuing further education or entering the workforce reflects positively on the quality of education provided by the school.

Evidence: Increased enrolment in higher education institutions and success stories of students post-graduation.

Teacher Effectiveness
Effective teaching practices contribute to positive perceptions of the school and its commitment to providing a high-quality education.

Evidence: High-quality teaching practices, innovation in instruction, and positive student-teacher relationships.

Professional Development Opportunities
A commitment to staff development demonstrates a proactive approach to maintaining high standards and adapting to educational advancements.

Evidence: Opportunities for staff to engage in ongoing professional development, training, and learning.

Community Engagement
Active engagement with the community suggests that the school fosters positive relationships and builds trust.

Evidence: Increased participation in school events, parent-teacher conferences, and community outreach programs.

Awards and Recognition
External validation through awards and recognitions positively influences the perception of the school's excellence.

Evidence: Receipt of awards, certifications, or recognition from educational organisations.

Technology Integration
Demonstrating a commitment to technological advancements contributes to the perception of a school as forward-thinking and adaptable.

Evidence: Effective technology integration in classrooms and innovative use of educational technology.

Parent and Student Satisfaction Surveys
High satisfaction levels indicate stakeholders perceive the school's changes as positive and effective.

Evidence: Positive feedback from parent and student satisfaction surveys.

Alumni Success Stories
Alumni success reflects positively on the school's ability to prepare students for future endeavours.

Evidence: Stories of alumni achieving success in their careers and personal lives.

Positive Media Coverage
Positive media coverage contributes to the external image and reputation of the school.

Evidence: Favourable media coverage, press releases, and positive news stories.

Increased Enrolment and Retention
A positive perception of the school attracts and retains students, contributing to a favourable reputation.

Evidence: A growing or stable student population with increased enrolment and retention rates.

Effective Communication Strategies
Effective communication fosters trust and understanding, positively influencing the school's reputation.

Evidence: Clear and transparent communication during organisational change.

Cultural Competence and Inclusivity
A commitment to fostering a diverse and inclusive environment positively influences the school's reputation.

Evidence: Initiatives promoting cultural competence, diversity, and inclusivity.

Financial Stability
Financial stability reflects positively on the school's management and contributes to a positive reputation.

Evidence: Demonstrated fiscal responsibility, effective financial management, and stewardship.

Monitoring these performance indicators provides evidence of the impact of organisational change on a school's reputation. Schools should use quantitative and qualitative data to assess their performance and make informed decisions to enhance their reputation within the educational community and the broader public.

49

Success Results

Maximising success in terms of a school's reputation during organisational change involves a strategic and intentional approach. Schools can take specific steps and considerations to optimise success results.

Clear Communication Strategy
Develop a clear and consistent communication strategy that outlines the reasons for the organisational change, the anticipated benefits, and the steps involved. Regularly update all stakeholders to maintain transparency and trust.

Highlight Positive Aspects
Emphasise the positive aspects and benefits of the organisational change. Clearly articulate how the change aligns with the school's mission, vision, and commitment to excellence in education.

Align with Stakeholder Values
Ensure that the organisational change aligns with the values and expectations of key stakeholders, including parents, teachers, students, and the wider community. Address concerns and demonstrate how the change supports shared goals.

Engage Stakeholders Actively
Actively involve stakeholders in the change process. Seek input, feedback, and ideas from teachers, parents, and students. Encourage participation in decision-making and implementation processes.

Leverage Success Stories
Share success stories and positive outcomes resulting from the organisational change. Highlight the achievements of students,

teachers, and the school community to showcase the positive impact of the change.

Utilise Media and Public Relations
Effectively leverage media channels and public relations to communicate success stories and positive developments related to the organisational change. Positive coverage can enhance the school's reputation.

Showcase Innovative Practices
Showcase innovative teaching practices, curriculum changes, or technological advancements that result from the organisational change. Demonstrate the school's commitment to staying at the forefront of education.

Maintain a Focus on Student Success
Demonstrate how the organisational change is directly contributing to improved student success. Highlight academic achievements, extracurricular accomplishments, and positive developments in students' personal growth.

Address Concerns Proactively
Proactively address any concerns or resistance to the organisational change. Provide forums for open dialogue, share information about the change process, and address misconceptions or uncertainties.

Involve Alumni in Promotions
Involve successful alumni who have benefited from the changes in promotional efforts. Alumni success stories can serve as powerful testimonials to the positive impact of the school's initiatives.

Celebrate Milestones and Achievements
Celebrate milestones and achievements related to the organisational change. Host events, ceremonies, or announcements to publicly acknowledge and recognise the efforts and progress made.

Demonstrate Adaptability
Emphasise the school's adaptability and responsiveness to changing educational landscapes. Showcase how the organisation proactively addresses emerging needs and prepares students for the future.

Engage with Educational Rankings
Participate in educational rankings and assessments that align with the school's goals. Positive rankings can contribute to the overall perception of the school's quality and effectiveness.

Promote Community Involvement
Highlight the school's commitment to community involvement and service. Showcase partnerships with local organisations, community events, and initiatives that contribute positively to the broader community.

Seek Accreditation and Endorsements
Pursue relevant accreditations and endorsements from educational bodies. These external validations can enhance the school's reputation and provide credibility to the organisational changes.

Utilise Digital Platforms
Leverage digital platforms and social media to share updates, success stories, and positive aspects of the organisational change. Engage with the online community to broaden the reach of the school's narrative.

Conduct Regular Reputation Audits
Conduct regular reputation audits to assess how the school is perceived both internally and externally. Use the insights to refine communication strategies and address areas that may impact reputation.

Sustain a Commitment to Excellence
Reinforce a commitment to excellence in education throughout the organisational change. Continuously strive for high standards, quality teaching, and positive learning outcomes to uphold and enhance the school's reputation.

By strategically implementing these measures, schools can actively contribute to the success of organisational change and maximise positive outcomes for their reputation. Throughout the change process, it's crucial to maintain a focus on continuous improvement, open communication, and a student-centric approach.

50
Success Inspiration

Maximising success and inspiration from organisational change in terms of a school's reputation involves intentional efforts to showcase positive outcomes and engage stakeholders effectively. Here are specific strategies to enhance success and inspiration from organisational change.

Craft a Compelling Narrative
Develop a compelling narrative that communicates the purpose, journey, and positive impact of the organisational change. Tell a story that resonates with stakeholders and highlights the school's commitment to continuous improvement.

Establish a Strong Vision
Clearly articulate a strong and inspiring vision for the school's future as a result of the organisational change. Align the vision with the values of the school community to create a shared sense of purpose.

Leadership Communication
Ensure that school leaders consistently communicate the vision, goals, and progress of the organisational change. Leadership should convey confidence, enthusiasm, and a genuine belief in the positive outcomes.

Highlight Transformational Practices
Showcase specific examples of transformational practices resulting from the organisational change. Highlight innovative teaching methods, student achievements, and unique programs contributing to the school's success.

Engage Student Ambassadors
Empower students to serve as ambassadors for the positive changes happening in the school. Student testimonials, projects, and success stories can be powerful tools to inspire confidence and pride.

Involve Parents in Celebrations
Involve parents in celebratory events and activities related to the organisational change. Host forums, presentations, or showcases where parents can witness and celebrate the positive impact on their children's education.

Create a Positive Atmosphere
Foster a positive and celebratory atmosphere within the school community. Host events, assemblies, or themed weeks that focus on the achievements and positive aspects of the organisational change.

Promote Team Success
Emphasise the collective success of the school community. Highlight collaborative efforts, teamwork, and the shared commitment to the organisational change, reinforcing a sense of pride and accomplishment.

Publicise Recognitions and Awards
Publicise any recognitions, awards, or accolades received as a result of the organisational change. Positive external validation contributes significantly to the school's reputation.

Showcase Community Impact
Demonstrate how the organisational change positively impacts the broader community. Highlight community service initiatives, partnerships, and projects that reflect the school's commitment to making a difference.

Leverage Alumni Success Stories
Share success stories of alumni who have thrived due to the school's programs and organisational changes. Alumni testimonials can inspire current students and improve the school's reputation.

Utilise Multimedia Platforms
Leverage multimedia platforms, including video testimonials, podcasts, and visual presentations, to effectively convey the success and inspiration behind the organisational change. Multimedia can engage and resonate with diverse audiences.

Host Inspiration Sessions
Organise inspiration sessions or workshops where stakeholders can hear firsthand accounts of the positive impact of the organisational change. Feature speakers, panels, or interactive sessions that celebrate success.

Engage with Social Media Campaigns
Develop strategic social media campaigns highlighting success stories, achievements, and positive aspects of the organisational change. Encourage community participation through hashtags and interactive content.

Offer Professional Development Opportunities
Showcase professional development opportunities for staff that have resulted from the organisational change. Highlight how these opportunities contribute to a culture of continuous learning and growth.

Conduct Open Houses and Showcases
Organise open houses or showcases where the school community, parents, and stakeholders can witness firsthand the positive changes within the school. Provide guided tours and presentations.

Encourage Peer Collaboration
Foster a culture of collaboration among educators by encouraging peer collaboration and sharing of successful practices. Celebrate examples of effective collaboration that emerged from the organisational change.

Promote a Culture of Celebration
Instil a culture of celebration and acknowledgment within the school. Regularly recognise and celebrate achievements, milestones, and positive contributions resulting from the organisational change.

By implementing these strategies, schools can effectively maximise success and inspiration from organisational change, contributing to a positive reputation within the school community and beyond. Continuous communication, celebration of achievements, and a focus on shared success can create a culture that inspires confidence and pride.

51
Promotion

Promoting the successful outcomes of organisational change in schools requires a strategic and thoughtful approach. School leaders can implement several key strategies to enhance the likelihood of successful organisational change.

Clearly Define Goals and Objectives
Clearly articulate the goals and objectives of the organisational change. Communicate the purpose and expected outcomes to all stakeholders, ensuring a shared understanding of the vision for change.

Engage Stakeholders from the Beginning
Involve key stakeholders, including teachers, staff, parents, and students, from the beginning stages of the change process. Solicit their input, feedback, and ideas to create a sense of ownership and collaboration.

Effective Communication
Establish a comprehensive communication plan that includes regular updates, transparent messaging, and opportunities for two-way communication. Ensure that information about the change is disseminated consistently and reaches all stakeholders.

Provide Professional Development
Offer relevant and targeted professional development opportunities for staff to build the skills and knowledge necessary to implement the change successfully. Through training programs, address any concerns or gaps in expertise.

Create a Positive School Culture
Foster a positive and supportive school culture that embraces change and innovation. Recognise and celebrate successes and encourage a growth mindset among staff and students.

Build Leadership Capacity
Develop leadership capacity at all levels within the school. Empower and train leaders to effectively guide and support their teams through the change process. Distributed leadership can help distribute responsibility and foster collaboration.

Establish Clear Implementation Plans
Develop detailed and realistic implementation plans with clear timelines and milestones. Break down the change into manageable phases, allowing for a structured and organised approach to implementation.

Promote Resources and Support
Ensure that the necessary resources, whether financial, technological, or human, are available to support the change initiative. Offer ongoing support to staff, addressing any challenges they may face during the implementation.

Monitor and Adjust
Implement mechanisms for monitoring progress and collecting feedback throughout the change process. Use this data to make informed adjustments to the implementation plan and address any emerging issues promptly.

Celebrate Small Wins
Acknowledge and celebrate small victories and milestones achieved during the change process. Recognising successes boosts morale and reinforces the positive aspects of the change.

Create a Feedback Loop
Establish a continuous feedback loop that allows stakeholders to share their thoughts, concerns, and suggestions. Act on feedback where possible and demonstrate that the organisation values input.

Align with School Mission and Values
Ensure that the organisational change aligns with the school's mission and core values. A clear connection between the change and the school's overarching goals can enhance commitment and understanding.

Encourage Creativity and Innovation
Foster a culture of innovation and creativity that encourages staff to explore new ideas and approaches. Provide opportunities for experimentation and learning from both successes and failures.

Promote Collaboration and Teamwork
Emphasise collaboration and teamwork throughout the change process. Encourage open communication and the sharing of ideas among staff members, fostering a sense of collective responsibility.

Address Resistance
Acknowledge and address resistance to change by providing opportunities for individuals to express their concerns. Offer support and resources to help individuals navigate and adapt to the changes.

Evaluate and Reflect
Regular evaluations of the change initiative should be conducted to assess its effectiveness. Reflect on the outcomes, lessons learned, and areas for improvement to inform future change efforts.

Sustain Momentum
Develop strategies to sustain the momentum generated by successful outcomes. Plan for the long-term sustainability of the changes and integrate them into the ongoing practices of the school.

Promote a Growth Mindset
Foster a growth mindset among both staff and students. Encourage a belief that challenges can be overcome through effort, learning, and resilience, promoting a positive attitude toward change.

By adopting these strategies, schools can create an environment conducive to successful organisational change. It's essential to recognise that change is a dynamic process, and ongoing efforts to engage stakeholders, communicate effectively, and adapt to emerging needs contribute to sustained success.

SECTION 8

FOCUS

Focus is like a superpower in the world of learning because it is the key to productivity, quality of work, essential for deep and meaningful learning and reduces stress by focusing on one task at a time.

— *Ken Darvall*

52
Student Engagement

Student engagement is a critical aspect of a successful educational environment, and addressing issues related to student engagement may require organisational change. Common student engagement issues may necessitate organisational change.

Lack of Relevance in Curriculum
Students may disengage if they find the curriculum irrelevant to their interests or future goals. Implement a review and revision of the curriculum to incorporate real-world applications, diverse perspectives, and project-based learning.

Inefficient Teaching Methods
Traditional or ineffective teaching methods may only interest some students. Provide professional development for teachers to incorporate varied and innovative teaching strategies, such as interactive lessons, technology integration, and differentiated instruction.

Limited Student Voice and Choice
Students may feel disengaged if they have little say in their learning experiences. Implement initiatives that promote student voice and choice, such as involving students in decision-making processes, offering elective courses, and incorporating student feedback into curriculum planning.

Insufficient Technology Integration
A lack of technology integration may result in disengagement, especially for students who are accustomed to digital learning. Invest in and integrate technology into classrooms, train teachers on tech tools, and create a digital learning environment.

Inadequate Support Services
Lack of support services for students facing academic, social, or emotional challenges. Establish or enhance support services such as counselling, tutoring, mentoring programs, and interventions for students with specific needs.

Unsupportive School Culture
A school culture that does not value or celebrate student achievements may lead to disengagement. Foster a positive and inclusive school culture through initiatives like student recognition programs, extracurricular activities, and a focus on social-emotional learning.

Limited Extracurricular Activities
Insufficient extracurricular activities may result in students feeling disconnected from school. Expand extracurricular offerings, clubs, sports, and leadership opportunities to cater to diverse interests.

Inflexible Scheduling
Inflexible scheduling may hinder students' ability to pursue their interests or manage their time effectively. Implement flexible scheduling options, such as block scheduling or blended learning, to accommodate diverse learning preferences and commitments.

High-Stakes Testing Pressure
Overemphasis on high-stakes testing can lead to student stress and disengagement. Advocate for balanced assessment practices, reduce the emphasis on standardised testing, and promote alternative forms of assessment that measure holistic student growth.

Inequitable Access to Resources
Disparities in resource access and educational opportunities may lead to disengagement among certain student populations. Implement policies and practices that address resource disparities,

including equitable distribution of materials, technology, and educational support services.

Bullying and Safety Concerns
Bullying, safety concerns, or an unwelcoming environment can negatively impact student engagement. Implement anti-bullying programs, enhance school safety measures, and foster a positive and inclusive school climate.

Limited Community Engagement
Lack of involvement from parents and the community may affect student engagement. Initiate programs encouraging parent and community involvement, such as family engagement events, community partnerships, and volunteer opportunities.

Addressing these student engagement issues often requires a multifaceted approach involving collaboration among educators, administrators, students, parents, and the broader community. Organisational change should be guided by a commitment to creating a positive, inclusive, and student-centred learning environment.

53
Curriculum for Choice

Common curriculum issues may require organisational change in a school.

Outdated Content
Curriculum content must be updated and align with current knowledge or societal needs. Regularly review and update curriculum content to ensure it is relevant, reflects advancements in knowledge, and addresses contemporary issues.

Lack of Diversity and Inclusivity
The curriculum lacks diversity in perspectives, cultures, and experiences, leading to a limited understanding of the world. Infuse diversity and inclusivity into the curriculum by incorporating materials, authors, and perspectives from a range of cultures, backgrounds, and identities.

Inflexible Structure
A rigid curriculum structure does not accommodate diverse learning styles and needs. Introduce flexibility in the curriculum structure, allowing for personalised learning, project-based approaches, and opportunities for student choice.

Limited Integration of Technology
The curriculum does not effectively leverage technology for teaching and learning. Implement strategies to integrate technology into the curriculum, provide professional development for teachers, and ensure access to digital resources.

Misalignment with Standards and Assessments
Misalignment between the curriculum, academic standards, and assessment methods. Align the curriculum with established

educational standards and ensure assessments measure the intended learning outcomes.

Insufficient Focus on Skills
The curriculum emphasises content knowledge over the development of essential skills, such as critical thinking, problem-solving, and communication. Integrate skill-based learning opportunities into the curriculum, emphasising the development of 21st-century skills.

Inadequate Preparation for Future Careers
The curriculum does not adequately prepare students for future careers and real-world challenges. Collaborate with industry partners, incorporate career-oriented learning experiences, and provide opportunities for skill development relevant to future employment.

Overemphasis on Standardised Testing
The curriculum focuses excessively on preparing students for standardised tests, potentially narrowing the educational experience. Advocate for a balanced approach to assessment, reducing reliance on standardised testing and emphasising formative assessments that inform instruction.

Lack of Interdisciplinary Connections
Siloed subject areas may not facilitate interdisciplinary connections and holistic understanding. Encourage interdisciplinary collaboration among teachers, design projects that span multiple disciplines, and promote a holistic understanding of knowledge.

Inadequate Support for Diverse Learners
The curriculum may not address the needs of diverse learners, including those with learning disabilities or English language learners. Implement inclusive teaching practices, provide resources and support for diverse learners, and offer professional development for teachers in differentiated instruction.

Lack of Real-World Application
The curriculum lacks connections to real-world applications, leading to disengagement. Make learning more relevant and meaningful for students by incorporating real-world examples, projects, and applications into the curriculum.

Limited Focus on Social-Emotional Learning
The curriculum may not address the social-emotional needs of students. Integrate social-emotional learning (SEL) into the curriculum, promoting emotional intelligence, self-awareness, and interpersonal skills.

Inconsistent Implementation
There may be inconsistencies in how the curriculum is implemented across classrooms or grade levels. Provide training and support for teachers to ensure consistent and effective curriculum implementation, fostering a shared understanding of instructional goals.

Resistance to Change
There may be resistance to curriculum changes from teachers, administrators, or other stakeholders. Foster a culture of collaboration and open communication, involve stakeholders in the decision-making process, and provide professional development to build capacity for change.

Addressing these curriculum issues often requires a collaborative and strategic approach involving input from teachers, administrators, parents, and other relevant stakeholders. A commitment to continuous improvement should guide organisational change and ensure a high-quality, relevant, and equitable education for all students.

54
Learning Environment

Creating a positive and effective learning environment is essential for the success and wellbeing of students. Addressing learning environment issues may require organisational change to foster a culture prioritising inclusivity, student engagement, and continuous improvement. Common learning environment issues that may necessitate organisational change include:

Ineffective Classroom Management
Challenges in maintaining a positive and orderly classroom environment can impact student behaviour and engagement. Provide professional development on effective classroom management strategies, establish clear behaviour expectations, and support teachers in creating a positive learning atmosphere.

Limited Student Engagement
Lack of engagement and participation among students can lead to reduced interest in learning. Implement student-centred teaching approaches, incorporate interactive and hands-on activities, and provide resources to enhance instructional engagement.

Inadequate Resources for Diverse Learning Styles
Insufficient resources and materials can fail to cater to diverse learning styles and preferences. Invest in a variety of instructional materials, provide professional development on differentiated instruction, and promote the use of multimedia resources to address diverse learning needs.

Classroom Design Challenges
Ineffective classroom layouts, furniture, or lighting can hinder student comfort and collaboration. Redesign classrooms to create

flexible and collaborative spaces, incorporate ergonomic furniture, and optimise lighting for a conducive learning environment.

Inequitable Access to Educational Tools
Disparities in access to educational tools, technology, and learning resources among students can affect their learning. Implement policies and initiatives to address resource inequities, provide equal access to technology, and ensure all students have the tools they need for effective learning.

Challenges in Differentiated Instruction
Difficulty in implementing differentiated instruction can hinder meeting the diverse needs of students in the same classroom. Provide training on differentiated instruction, support teachers in adapting lessons to individual learning levels, and encourage collaboration among educators to share effective practices.

Ineffective Assessment Practices
Overreliance on traditional assessment methods may not accurately measure student understanding and growth. Promote a variety of assessment methods, including formative assessments, project-based assessments, and alternative assessments that align with learning objectives.

Limited Social-Emotional Learning Integration
Inadequate integration of social-emotional learning into the curriculum, impacting students' emotional intelligence and well-being. Infuse SEL into the curriculum, provide training for educators on fostering emotional intelligence, and create a positive and supportive school culture.

Unsupportive School Culture
A school culture does not promote inclusivity, respect, or a sense of belonging for all students. Foster a positive and inclusive school culture through leadership initiatives, professional development on cultural competence, and the implementation of anti-bias education.

Inefficient Use of Technology
Technology is not effectively integrated into the learning environment, leading to missed opportunities for interactive and collaborative learning. Provide professional development on technology integration, ensure access to appropriate digital resources, and support teachers in using technology to enhance instruction.

Limited Opportunities for Student Voice and Choice
Insufficient opportunities for students to express their opinions, interests, and preferences in their learning experiences can lead to disengagement. Implement strategies for student voice and choice, involve students in decision-making processes, and provide opportunities for project-based and inquiry-based learning.

Inadequate Support for Special Education
Insufficient support and resources for students with special needs can impact their ability to fully participate in the learning environment. Enhance support services for special education, provide professional development for inclusive practices, and ensure accessibility in the learning environment.

Limited Parent and Community Engagement
Insufficient involvement of parents and the community in the learning environment can hinder the establishment of a collaborative educational community. Develop strategies to enhance parental and community engagement, create opportunities for involvement, and communicate the importance of a collaborative educational community.

Unaddressed Bullying and Safety Concerns
Unaddressed bullying or safety concerns can create a hostile or unsafe learning environment. Implement anti-bullying programs, establish clear safety protocols, and create a culture of respect and inclusivity to ensure a safe and supportive learning environment.

Inconsistent Professional Learning Communities
Lack of consistent professional learning communities (PLCs) for educators to collaborate and share best practices can impede professional growth. Promote the establishment of PLCs, provide time and resources for collaborative planning, and foster a culture of continuous professional development.

Organisational changes to address learning environment issues should be informed by a comprehensive assessment of the educational institution's current state, including input from educators, students, parents, and the wider community. The changes should focus on creating an environment that supports students' holistic development, fosters a positive culture of learning, and encourages collaboration among all stakeholders.

55
Individualised Support

Individualised support refers to personalised assistance provided to meet the unique needs of individuals, particularly in the context of education or social services. Common issues related to individualised support may require organisational change.

Limited Personalisation in Education
One-size-fits-all approaches do not cater to the diverse needs, learning styles, and abilities of individual students. Implement strategies for personalised learning, such as differentiated instruction, flexible pacing, and tailored educational plans.

Inadequate Special Education Services
Insufficient support and resources for students with special needs, including those with learning disabilities or developmental challenges, can hinder their progress. Enhance special education programs, provide professional development for educators, and ensure the availability of necessary accommodations and resources.

Limited English Language Learning (ELL) Support
Inadequate support for students who are English language learners can hinder their language development and academic progress. Develop and implement effective English as a Second Language (ESL) programs, offer targeted language support, and promote a culturally responsive learning environment.

Challenges in Gifted and Talented Education
Inequities or insufficient support for gifted and talented students who may require advanced or specialised educational opportunities can limit their potential. Implement or enhance gifted education

programs, provide enrichment activities, and offer acceleration options to challenge high-achieving students.

Behavioural and Emotional Support Needs
Inadequate support for students with behavioural or emotional challenges can impact their overall wellbeing and academic success. Implement a multi-tiered system of support (MTSS), provide social-emotional learning programs, and offer counselling services to address the diverse needs of students.

Insufficient Support for Students with Trauma
Lack of trauma-informed practices and support for students who have experienced trauma can affect their ability to learn and engage in the educational environment. Implement trauma-informed training for staff, create a supportive and understanding school culture, and provide counselling services to address the impact of trauma.

Inequities in Access to Resources
Disparities in access to educational resources and support services can contribute to inequities in academic outcomes. Address resource inequities, implement policies to ensure equal access, and provide additional support to students facing socio-economic challenges.

Inconsistent Parental Involvement
Inconsistent or limited involvement of parents or guardians in the education and support of their children can affect student outcomes. Develop strategies to enhance parental engagement, such as family outreach programs, workshops, and effective communication channels.

Limited Career Guidance and Counselling
Inadequate support for students in making informed decisions about their future careers and educational paths. Enhance career guidance programs, provide counselling services, and establish

partnerships with industry professionals to expose students to diverse career options.

Challenges in Transition Planning
Inadequate planning and support for students transitioning between educational levels (e.g., from middle school to high school) or from school to post-school settings. Develop comprehensive transition plans, involve students in the planning process, and provide the necessary resources and support for successful transitions.

Insufficient Access to Assistive Technology
Limited access to assistive technology for students with disabilities hinders their participation and progress. Invest in assistive technology resources, provide training for educators, and ensure that technology is accessible to all students.

Data Privacy and Security Concerns
Concerns related to the privacy and security of student information, especially when implementing personalised learning technologies. Develop and communicate clear policies on data privacy, implement secure systems, and provide training to ensure compliance with data protection regulations.

Inflexible Assessment Practices
Assessment practices that do not accommodate the diverse needs and abilities of individual students. Implement flexible assessment methods, such as alternative assessments, accommodations, and differentiated evaluation approaches.

Inadequate Training for Educators
Insufficient training for educators to address the diverse needs of individual students, particularly in terms of special education and differentiated instruction. Provide ongoing professional development opportunities for educators to enhance their skills in meeting the individualised needs of students.

Limited Collaboration Among Support Staff
Lack of collaboration among support staff, including special education teachers, counsellors, and other specialists. Foster a collaborative culture among staff members, promote interdisciplinary collaboration, and establish regular communication channels to address student needs comprehensively.

Organisational change to address individualised support issues requires a commitment to inclusivity, equity, and continuous improvement. It often involves policy development, resource allocation, professional development, and cultural shifts within the educational institution.

56
Emotional Wellbeing

Addressing emotional wellbeing issues in an organisation, particularly in educational settings, may involve organisational changes to create a supportive and nurturing environment. Common emotional wellbeing issues that may necessitate organisational change include:

High Stress and Burnout Among Staff
Elevated stress levels and burnout among teachers and staff, impacting their mental well-being and effectiveness. Implement strategies for staff wellbeing, such as wellness programs, professional development on stress management, and workload assessment.

Insufficient Mental Health Support
Inadequate resources and support for addressing the mental health needs of students and staff. Establish or enhance mental health support services, provide training for educators, and promote a stigma-free environment for seeking help.

Bullying and Harassment
Incidents of bullying and harassment among students or staff negatively impact the emotional wellbeing of those involved. Implement anti-bullying programs, promote a culture of respect, and establish clear policies for addressing and preventing harassment.

Limited Social-Emotional Learning (SEL) Integration
Insufficient integration of social-emotional learning into the curriculum can lead to challenges in emotional regulation and interpersonal skills. Integrate SEL programs into the curriculum,

provide professional development for educators, and create a positive and inclusive school culture.

Inadequate Resources for Coping with Trauma
Lack of resources and support for students and staff who have experienced trauma can impact their emotional well-being. Develop trauma-informed practices, provide training for staff, and establish support systems for individuals affected by trauma.

Crisis-Response Preparedness
Inadequate preparation and response strategies for crises or emergencies can affect the emotional well-being of the school community. Develop and regularly update crisis response plans, conduct drills, and provide training for staff to handle crises.

Isolation and Lack of Community
Feelings of isolation among students, staff, or parents can lead to a lack of connection and support. Foster a sense of community through initiatives like mentorship programs, community events, and open communication channels.

Stigma Around Mental Health
Stigma or reluctance to discuss mental health concerns openly can hinder help-seeking behaviour. Promote mental health awareness campaigns, provide education on reducing stigma, and establish confidential avenues for seeking support.

Inequities in Access to Support Services
Disparities in access to mental health and well-being support services, particularly for marginalised or underserved populations. Address resource inequities, implement outreach programs, and ensure that support services are accessible to all students and staff.

Inadequate Parental Involvement in Emotional Wellbeing
Limited parental involvement in addressing the emotional well-being of their children. Provide resources and workshops for

parents on supporting their children's emotional wellbeing, and establish effective communication channels between parents and school staff.

Limited Focus on Mindfulness and Wellbeing Practices
Insufficient emphasis on mindfulness and wellbeing practices that promote stress reduction and emotional resilience. Integrate mindfulness programs, provide training for educators, and create dedicated spaces for relaxation and reflection.

Challenges in Building Resilience
Insufficient emphasis on building resilience skills among students and staff to cope with challenges. Implement programs and activities focusing on building resilience, such as character education, leadership development, and peer support initiatives.

Inconsistent Communication Channels
Inconsistent or ineffective communication channels can contribute to misunderstandings and stress. Enhance communication strategies, establish clear channels for information sharing, and encourage open dialogue among all stakeholders.

Lack of Training on Emotional Regulation
Limited training on emotional regulation for students can lead to challenges in managing emotions and conflicts. Integrate emotional regulation training into the curriculum, provide teacher resources, and create a supportive environment for students to express and manage their emotions.

Organisational changes to address emotional wellbeing issues should be holistic, involving collaboration among educators, administrators, students, parents, and mental health professionals. Creating a supportive and nurturing environment requires ongoing commitment, education, and the implementation of evidence-based practices that prioritise the emotional wellbeing of the entire school community.

57

Community Involvement

Community involvement is crucial for the success and effectiveness of educational institutions. Addressing community involvement may require organisational change to enhance collaboration, communication, and partnerships.

Limited Parental Engagement
Low parental involvement in school activities, decision-making processes, and student learning. Implement strategies to encourage parental engagement, such as regular communication, parent-teacher conferences, and involvement in school events.

Ineffective Communication Channels
Inadequate or ineffective communication between the school and the community leads to misunderstandings and reduced community engagement. Enhance communication strategies, utilise multiple channels (e.g., newsletters, social media, school websites), and establish clear lines of communication with the community.

Lack of Cultural Competence
Need for more understanding and incorporation of diverse cultural perspectives in school activities and communication. Provide cultural competency training for staff, promote inclusivity in school practices, and celebrate cultural diversity within the school community.

Limited Community Partnerships
Few or ineffective partnerships between the school and local organisations, businesses, or community groups. Actively seek and establish partnerships with community organisations,

businesses, and local leaders, fostering collaborations that benefit the school and the community.

Inequitable Access to Resources
Disparities in access to educational resources and opportunities among different community segments. Implement policies and initiatives to address resource inequities, ensuring that all community members have equal access to educational resources and opportunities.

Resistance to Change
Resistance from the community or school staff to changes in community engagement practices. Facilitate open dialogue with stakeholders, communicate the benefits of changes, and involve the community in decision-making processes to build support for organisational changes.

Limited Outreach to Underserved Communities
Inadequate outreach to underserved or marginalised communities, leading to a lack of representation and participation. Develop targeted outreach programs, engage with community leaders, and ensure that the needs of all community members are considered in decision-making processes.

Ineffective Volunteer Programs
Ineffective or underutilised volunteer programs that fail to harness community members' skills and resources. Assess and redesign volunteer programs, provide clear guidelines for participation, and recognise and appreciate the contributions of volunteers.

Lack of Community Input into Decision-Making
Limited opportunities for community members to provide input and feedback in school decision-making processes. Establish mechanisms for community input, such as advisory committees, town hall meetings, and surveys, to involve community members in shaping school policies and initiatives.

Insufficient Community Awareness
Lack of awareness in the community about school activities, achievements, and initiatives. Develop and implement marketing and communication strategies to raise awareness about school events, successes, and ongoing initiatives within the community.

Challenges in Engaging Diverse Stakeholders
Difficulty in engaging diverse stakeholders, including parents, community leaders, and local organisations, in school activities. Implement targeted engagement strategies, acknowledge and respect diverse perspectives, and actively seek input from various community stakeholders.

Inaccessible School Facilities
Limited access to school facilities for community use outside of regular school hours. Review and revise policies related to facility use, promote community access to school facilities, and establish guidelines for community use agreements.

Lack of Community Events
Infrequent or limited community events bring school staff, students, and community members together. Plan and organise regular community events, such as open houses, fairs, and forums, to foster positive interactions and collaboration.

Unwelcoming School Environment
Certain community members may perceive a school environment as unwelcoming or exclusive. Foster a culture of inclusivity, promote a welcoming atmosphere, and actively address any issues that contribute to this perception.

Inconsistent Community Engagement Strategies
Inconsistency or lack of coherence in community engagement strategies can lead to confusion and reduced effectiveness. Develop a comprehensive community engagement plan, align

strategies with overall school goals, and ensure consistency in communication and outreach efforts.

Organisational changes to address community involvement issues should be collaborative, transparent, and reflective of the community's needs and values. Effective community engagement contributes to a positive school culture and fosters a sense of shared responsibility for student success.

58
Technology Integration

Effective technology integration in educational organisations is crucial for providing modern and engaging learning experiences. Addressing technology integration issues may require organisational change to create a supportive infrastructure and a culture that embraces technological advancements.

Limited Access to Technology
Unequal access to technology devices and resources among students and staff. Implement initiatives to provide equitable access to technology, secure funding for device acquisition, and establish policies for responsible device use.

Inadequate Technology Infrastructure
Insufficient or outdated technology infrastructure, including networks, Wi-Fi, and servers. Invest in upgrading technology infrastructure, ensure scalability, and provide ongoing maintenance and support.

Inconsistent Professional Development
Lack of consistent and effective professional development opportunities for educators to enhance their technology skills. Develop a comprehensive professional development program, offer ongoing training, and incentivise educators to acquire and apply technology skills in their teaching practices.

Resistance to Change
Resistance from educators, administrators, or staff to incorporating new technologies into teaching and learning. Foster a culture of innovation, support change through training and mentorship, and recognise and celebrate successful technology integration initiatives.

Ineffective Integration into Curriculum
Technology is being used as an add-on rather than being fully integrated into the curriculum to enhance learning outcomes. Revise curriculum frameworks to include technology integration, guide embedding technology into lesson plans, and encourage interdisciplinary projects that leverage technology.

Lack of Digital Literacy Skills
Need for more digital literacy skills among students and educators to navigate and critically evaluate online information. Implement digital literacy programs, integrate information literacy into the curriculum, and offer training on responsible and ethical technology use.

Digital Privacy Concerns
Concerns about student and staff data privacy and security when using technology tools and platforms. Develop and communicate clear data privacy policies, provide data protection training, and ensure compliance with relevant regulations.

Inconsistent Tech Support
Inconsistent or inadequate technical support for troubleshooting and resolving technology-related issues. Enhance technical support services, train in-house support personnel, and establish clear communication channels for reporting and addressing technical issues.

Limited Parent and Community Involvement
Limited engagement of parents and the community in understanding and supporting technology integration initiatives. Develop communication strategies to inform parents and the community about technology initiatives, provide training opportunities, and create forums for collaboration and feedback.

Overemphasis on Hardware
There may be an overemphasis on acquiring hardware without a corresponding focus on software, digital content, and pedagogical strategies. Adopt a balanced approach that considers hardware and software needs, invests in educational software, and aligns technology purchases with instructional goals.

Limited Tech Integration in Assessment
Technology is not effectively integrated into assessment practices, leading to traditional assessment methods that may not fully capture 21st-century skills. Explore and implement technology-enhanced assessment methods, provide training on digital assessment tools, and align assessments with desired learning outcomes.

Inadequate Digital Citizenship Education
There is a lack of emphasis on teaching students about responsible and ethical behaviour in digital environments. Integrate digital citizenship education into the curriculum, provide resources for educators, and promote a culture of responsible digital behaviour.

Insufficient Collaboration Tools
There is a lack of effective collaboration tools for educators and students to work together on projects and assignments. Implement and promote collaboration tools, such as online platforms and communication apps, to facilitate teamwork and communication.

Technology-Driven Inequities
Technological initiatives may contribute to disparities in educational opportunities and outcomes. Develop strategies to address technology-driven inequities, provide additional support for underserved populations, and ensure that technology enhances inclusivity.

Inadequate Budget Allocation
There are inadequate budget allocations for technology integration, limiting the ability to acquire necessary devices, software, and training. Advocate for adequate funding, align budget priorities with technology goals, and explore external funding opportunities.

Organisational changes to address technology integration issues should be strategic, collaborative, and focused on creating an environment that values innovation and embraces technology's benefits in education. This requires a commitment to ongoing professional development, infrastructure improvement, and a culture encouraging experimentation and adaptation to technological advancements.

59
Extracurricular

Common extracurricular issues that may necessitate organisational change in a school can vary, but they often revolve around enhancing the effectiveness, inclusivity, and overall experience of extracurricular activities.

Limited Participation
There is low student participation in extracurricular activities. Implement strategies to increase awareness, promote diverse activities, and create incentives for student involvement.

Lack of Diversity and Inclusivity
There is a lack of diversity and inclusivity in extracurricular programs. Introduce new activities that cater to a broader range of interests, ensure representation in leadership roles, and promote a culture of inclusivity.

Insufficient Resources
There are limited resources for extracurricular programs, including funding, space, and equipment. Explore alternative funding sources, establish partnerships with local businesses or community organisations, and optimise the use of existing resources.

Ineffective Communication
There is poor communication about extracurricular opportunities, events, and updates. Improve communication channels, utilise digital platforms, and establish a centralised system for disseminating information to students, parents, and staff.

Inadequate Supervision and Mentorship
There is a lack of effective supervision and mentorship for extracurricular activities.

Implement mentorship programs, provide supervisor training, and ensure adequate staffing to support each activity's needs.

Outdated or Inflexible Programs
Extracurricular programs may be outdated or inflexible. Review and update existing programs, introduce new activities that align with current interests and trends, and allow for flexibility in program structure.

Limited Accessibility
Extracurricular activities may not be easily accessible to all students. Ensure that activities are scheduled at times convenient for a diverse student body, provide transportation options, and remove barriers to participation.

Student Burnout
Students may experience burnout due to an overwhelming number of extracurricular commitments. Implement guidelines for reasonable levels of involvement, promote a balanced approach to academics and extracurriculars, and offer support for students struggling with time management.

Evaluation and Recognition Challenges
There may be a lack of a structured system for evaluating and recognising achievements in extracurricular activities. Develop clear criteria for evaluating participation and accomplishments, establish a recognition program, and celebrate student achievements regularly.

Alignment with Educational Goals
Extracurricular activities may not be aligned with the school's educational goals and values. Activities should complement the

school's mission, contribute to students' overall development, and align with educational objectives.

Stakeholder Engagement
There may be a lack of involvement of parents, teachers, and community members in supporting and promoting extracurricular activities. Foster greater collaboration with stakeholders, create volunteer opportunities, and organise events that involve the broader community.

Technology Integration
There may be a lack of integration of technology in extracurricular programs. Explore ways to incorporate technology for enhanced learning experiences, virtual participation, and communication.

Addressing these issues through strategic organisational change can contribute to a more vibrant, inclusive, and effective extracurricular environment within the school. It's important to involve key stakeholders, gather feedback, and continuously assess the impact of changes to ensure ongoing improvement.

60
School Expertise

Staff expertise is crucial in the success of organisational change within a school setting. Here are several key reasons highlighting the importance of staff expertise during times of change.

Knowledge of the School Environment
Staff members have a deep understanding of the school's culture, history, and current environment. Their expertise is invaluable in navigating the unique challenges and opportunities associated with the school's specific context.

Insight into Student Needs
Teachers and other staff interact directly with students, enabling them to understand the student body's needs, preferences, and learning styles. This insight is critical when implementing changes that directly impact the student experience.

Operational Understanding
Staff members are familiar with the school's day-to-day operations. Their expertise ensures a realistic assessment of proposed changes' feasibility and potential impact on various aspects of school operations, including scheduling, resource allocation, and logistical considerations.

Instructional Delivery and Design
Teachers bring expertise in instructional design and delivery. Their insights into effective teaching methodologies, curriculum design, and assessment practices are essential for aligning organisational changes with educational goals and standards.

Leadership and Mentorship
Experienced staff often serve as informal leaders and mentors within the school community. Their leadership skills and mentorship can help guide colleagues through the change process, provide support, share best practices, and foster a positive culture.

Cultural Knowledge and Sensitivity
Staff members are attuned to the school's cultural nuances and the dynamics of relationships within the community. This cultural knowledge is crucial for implementing changes in a way that respects existing traditions, values, and relationships.

Effective Communication
Staff expertise contributes to effective communication during organisational change. Teachers, administrators, and support staff are familiar with the most effective communication channels within the school community, ensuring that messages are conveyed clearly and reach all stakeholders.

Problem-Solving Skills
Staff members, especially those with experience, have honed problem-solving skills through their years of service. This expertise is valuable when addressing challenges and overcoming obstacles that may arise during the change process.

Buy-In and Commitment
Involving staff in the change process leverages their expertise, fosters a sense of ownership, and increases buy-in. When staff members understand the rationale behind the changes and see their input valued, they are more likely to commit to and actively support the change efforts.

Professional Development Opportunities
Staff expertise contributes to the identification of relevant professional development opportunities. Understanding the

skill sets needed for successful implementation of changes enables schools to provide targeted training that enhances staff capabilities.

Evaluation and Feedback
Staff expertise is instrumental in developing meaningful evaluation metrics and providing constructive feedback. Their input ensures that the impact of organisational change is assessed accurately, allowing for adjustments and improvements as needed.

Cohesive Team Dynamics
A team of skilled and experienced staff can foster cohesive team dynamics during periods of change. Their collective expertise contributes to a collaborative and supportive atmosphere, where colleagues work together to achieve common goals.

Continuity and Stability
Staff continuity provides stability during periods of change. Retaining experienced staff members helps maintain institutional memory, ensuring that lessons learned from past experiences contribute to the success of the current change initiative.

Adaptability and Innovation
Experienced staff members bring adaptability and innovation to the change process. Their familiarity with different instructional methods, technologies, and pedagogical approaches allows for creative solutions and exploring new strategies.

Cultural Alignment and Change
Staff members who are culturally aligned with the goals of organisational change are more likely to contribute positively to the process. Their expertise in aligning the change with the existing culture helps create a smoother transition.

In summary, staff expertise is a valuable resource contributing to the success of school organisational change. By leveraging the knowledge, skills, and insights of experienced staff members, schools can navigate change more effectively, ensuring that the process is well-informed, student-centred, and aligned with the broader educational mission.

www.ingramcontent.com/pod-product-compliance
Lightning Source LLC
Chambersburg PA
CBHW041138110526
44590CB00027B/4059